W9-BXZ-127

SUPPORTED BY **TATE MEMBERS**
AND **TATE ST IVES' MEMBERS**   PUBLISHED BY   TATE ^{St IVES}

ON THE VERY EDGE OF THE OCEAN

The Porthmeor Studios and Painting in St Ives

BEN TUFNELL

Tate St Ives
RESEARCH SERIES

Contents

Foreword

In Appreciation
SUSAN DANIEL

On June 3 2006, more than 300 guests packed into Studio number three of the historic Porthmeor Studios to hear the broadcaster Janet Street Porter launch a community fundraising day called The Smart Regeneration (of Porthmeor Studios), organised by Jane Val Baker. The Borlase Smart-John Wells Trust, as it became known in 2002–03, which manages the studios, had raised £1.2M from the Arts Council of England South West to renovate the large labyrinthine building on the edge of Porthmeor Beach and preserve its historic nature for future generations of artists and fishermen who will be drawn to work in St Ives. The appeal for £100,000 from the community is set in the context of an overall project cost of £2.7M and has captured the imagination of many visitors and local artists, fishermen, friends and members of the St Ives community, highlighting the important place Porthmeor Studios has in the collective memory of those connected with both the artistic and the fishing community.

In its heyday, at the high points in the development of the artistic colony in St Ives – in the late nineteenth century and after the second World War – Porthmeor Studios were considered to be the apogee of cultural practice and bohemia, attracting some artists to the art historical context and the unique light, some to work in the cheap and unconventionally large studios next to the ocean, and some to the parties. Today the studios are as important and alive as they ever were with one third of the spaces occupied by young artists and the Tate St Ives Residency Programme bringing a new encumbent to the studios every six to nine months. The fact that artists and fishermen work together in harmony is unique amongst all the studio buildings in Britain and when the renovation is completed in

2010, the tenants in this unique building will continue to work in protected circumstances on the very edge of the Atlantic Ocean.

This publication marks an important piece of research commissioned by Tate St Ives in 2004 and is published in the year in which the Trust is working to realise the funding for building work to begin in 2008 for completion in 2010.

I am particularly grateful to Tate St Ives Members for financially supporting this research and publication, bringing new knowledge into existence on this important aspect of the St Ives story. I am indebted to the artists in Porthmeor Studios for readily making themselves available for interviews with Ben Tufnell assisted by Sara Hughes. We appreciate the conservation and care of the Borlase Smart-John Wells Trust archive files by Cath Wallace – previously Administrator of the Trust – and Chris Hibbert, the current Manager, as well as the Arts Council of England. As always, members of the TSI team have been closely involved in this production; Kerry Rice, Arwen Fitch, Alex Lambley, Fiona Cattrell and Sara Hughes. Judith Severne at Tate Publishing has been a constant support throughout the editing process.

I am grateful to local historian and Honorary Curator of the St Ives Museum, Brian Stevens for his unique text on the history and workings of the Porthmeor Studio cellars occupied by the fishermen of St Ives. Finally my warm thanks to Curator and author Ben Tufnell for his inspirational energy and extended commitment to this project and his insightful text which brings new knowledge to the St Ives context.

Acknowledgements

Many people have given invaluable assistance in the making of this book. At Tate I would like to thank Susan Daniel, Director of Tate St Ives, who commissioned this research supported by Tate St Ives Members and has continued to give crucial advice and support; Sara Hughes, Curator at Tate St Ives, who has given important research help as well as overseeing the production of the book; Chris Stephens, Senior Curator, Tate Britain, who has been very generous in sharing his knowledge of St Ives and commented on an early draft of the text. In addition, I would like to thank Stephen Deuchar, Judith Nesbitt and Christine Riding for their support.

I am particularly indebted to the artists who worked at Porthmeor who took the time to discuss the studios with me: Trevor Bell, Bob Crossley, John Emanuel, Patrick Hughes, Sax Impey, John Mitchell, Breon O'Casey, Jane O'Malley, Ged Quinn and Roy Ray. Before his death in 2004 I enjoyed many fascinating discussions with Karl Weschke. I am immensely grateful to him for his friendship.

In addition, warm thanks are due to: Michael Bird and Ross Brody who provided important research assistance; Kate Austin, Janet Axten, Gerard Faggionato, Katharine Heron and Julian Feary, Ysanne Holt, Chris Redgrave, Judith Severne, David Tovey, Cath Wallace, Petronilla Weschke, and the staff at the Arts Council Archive and Tate Archive and Library.

Finally, I would like to thank Cecilia and Pablo who have done so much to distract me from the research and the writing. This book is for them.

BEN TUFNELL

On the very Edge of the Ocean

The Porthmeor Studios and Painting in St Ives

BEN TUFNELL

**View of Porthmeor
Studios from the beach**
Photo: Marcus Leith and
Andrew Dunkley
© Tate

1   Introduction

Where else in the country are there 13 studios, with a total floor space of over 8,200 square feet, placed at the same time at the centre of a painting community and (most dramatically) on the very edge of the ocean, where in consequence, the light is of a brilliance that is unique in England?

Patrick Heron, letter to Robin Campbell, 1975

Here in front of the wide, high studio window lie the rocks and the sands of the beach, the sun rises and sets in splendour to the tune of the Atlantic waves, sometimes meditative, sometimes agitated, never calm. When the autumn and spring gales whip the waters to a frenzy they reveal the fury of the elements with such undirected power that the artist in his studio, with his coal-burning iron stove as his only companion, finds peace for his mind and shelter for his working.

J.P. Hodin, *Douglas Portway: A Painter's Life,* 1983[1]

Any account of the Porthmeor Studios must begin with Porthmeor Beach, the most westerly of the four beaches of St Ives. A magnificent stretch of pale sand, the beach is about a quarter of a mile across and bounded on the west by Man's Head and on the east by The Island. These two promontories frame the view from the beach out to the Atlantic and, as Matthew Rowe has observed, lend it a 'peculiarly rectangular and deep aerial plane'.[2] In the summer, when the sun is out, the beach shines brightly and the water takes on the translucent aquamarine hues we more readily associate with the Mediterranean. The light is dazzling. In winter, on a calm day, the water can look like metal and the reflected light on the wet sand sometimes creates the illusion that land and sea and water and sky elide one into another in a single unbroken plane. In inclement weather turbulent seas and huge waves crash against the sand. The beach and the great Atlantic rollers that break along its length are popular with surfers.

When tourists first started to come to St Ives, Porthmeor Beach was largely ignored. In the late nineteenth century and first half of the twentieth century the harbour was the focus of the town and Porthminster and Porthgwidden Beaches were popular for bathing: Porthmeor was associated with the old fishing quarter and was dominated by the gasworks. Yet since the Second World War Porthmeor and the view of the Atlantic from the beach have come to be seen as somehow offering an emblematic aspect of St Ives. A large part of this has been to do with the artists who have occupied the buildings that line the back of the eastern end of the beach, along Back Road West; where in the last two decades of the nineteenth century old net lofts were rented or bought cheaply and converted into studios. It is here the Porthmeor Studios are located, overlooking the beach. Artists have been in residence since the 1880s, and the defining aspect of their occupation of this studio complex has been the extraordinary view – of sand and sea and sky – framed by the large windows installed on the seaward side of the building.

Positioned, as Patrick Heron noted, 'on the very edge of the ocean', an inescapable daily fact of any working life in these studios has been the direct observation of raw, ever-changing nature; rhythmic, threatening, elemental, dissolving. Inevitably this has been reflected in the art made here.

The Porthmeor Studios are ramshackle and labyrinthine. At their western end, steps lead up from Back Road West to two huge studios on the first floor, with tall ceilings going up into the rafters of the building and wide high windows on the seaward side. These are No.1, which Borlase Smart occupied for twenty years from 1924 to 1944, and No.2, where John Emanuel has worked since 1983. Below, a ramp runs down from the road to a gate beneath an arch, passing the doors to Nos.3, 4 and 5. No.3 is a long low-ceilinged studio, where Francis Bacon worked in the winter of 1959. No.4 was Terry Frost's studio for most of the 1950s. No.5 is at the heart of the complex and has been occupied variously by such major figures as Julius Olsson, Ben Nicholson and Patrick Heron. It is currently the location for the Tate St Ives Artist's Residency programme.

Through the gate is a small courtyard filled with boxes of nets, colourful floats, ropes and other fishing paraphernalia. From here it is clear that the buildings, like many in St Ives, have been constructed in an unplanned and haphazard style. From the courtyard there is access to some of the cellars beneath the studios, which are still used by fishermen for the storage and maintenance of their equipment. Facing the entrance to the yard is the doorway to No.9, up a short flight of steps. A second flight of steps to the left leads up to the door of No.8 and a short passageway. Here are the doors to Nos.6 and 7, where Frances Hodgkins lived and worked during the First World War.

Further along Back Road West, passing a private house surrounded by the studios on three sides, one reaches two more doors and another flight of steps. The left-hand door leads into the offices of the St Ives School of Painting. The second door opens onto a short passageway that leads to No.12, the smallest studio and No.10, occupied by Hyman Segal from 1948 until his death in 2004, which is situated directly above No.9. The wooden steps lead up to No.11, a large airy studio with windows on both sides, where the St Ives School of Painting has conducted its classes since 1938.

It is an extraordinary complex of buildings. The walls and floors wear a rich patina of history, the marks left by a succession of tenants. Since they were first converted to studios over a century ago they have been in continuous use – by both painters and sculptors – and have frequently been used as homes as well as workspaces. However, the studios themselves are worn and dilapidated; some are almost decrepit. The roofs leak. There is damp. Many of the windows are broken and patched. The walls are cracked. For more than 150 years they have been battered by the harsh Atlantic weather and are now in urgent need of attention.

Despite an unprepossessing exterior, there are a number of reasons why the studios have long been coveted by artists. As spaces they are bigger than almost any other in St Ives – a town characterised by small rooms – allowing an artist to work on a scale that could not be achieved elsewhere. Furthermore, here one is positioned at the centre of the local art colony. At Porthmeor one might work in close proximity to a peer group consisting of many of the most important artists working in the town at any one time, thus opening up opportunities for mutual support and encouragement. For example, Terry Frost has spoken of how he and Ben Nicholson, who occupied Nos.4 and 5 respectively in the early 1950s, would visit each other's studios on a daily basis and offer criticism and advice on work in progress. For Frost, then in the early stages of his career, contact and support from such an established artist as Nicholson was very important.

Porthmeor was well known as a centre for art. At least five art schools have been run from the studios, three of which – Julius Olsson's, the St Ives School of Painting and St Peter's Loft – are of real significance

Julius Olsson (1864–1942)
Moonlight on Breakers
Oil on canvas
70 × 90cm
© Private Collection
Image courtesy of
Jordan & Chard Fine Art

for the development of the colony. Many of the artists who eventually settled in St Ives first visited to attend one of these schools. By the late 1920s and 1930s Nos.4 and 5 served as a gallery for the St Ives Society of Artists, with regular exhibitions of members' work. The Porthmeor Studios block was therefore a popular destination for visitors to the town. With a studio opening straight onto the street an artist might expect large numbers of visitors, and corresponding opportunities to sell work. When William Redgrave first moved into No.12 in spring 1952 he was told by Hyman Segal that he received thousands of visitors a year to his studio. For Redgrave, this promised the prospect of sales and he anticipated that this would be an important source of income.

Porthmeor is not the only studio complex in St Ives, but is probably the longest established and certainly the most important. The studios were almost certainly built in the mid-nineteenth century as part of a complex of net lofts that extended the length of Downalong, the old fishing quarter of St Ives. At ground level the Porthmeor buildings had (and still have) extensive pilchard tanks for the storage of salted fish. Above they have high airy ceilings for the drying of nets. When artists began to come to St Ives in the 1880s, the net or fish lofts were an obvious choice for conversion into studios. It was relatively simple to let in skylights and large windows and whitewash the spaces. Not only was their scale ideal; they faced north, giving perfect light for painting, and commanded extraordinary views, being right by the sea. From very early on, accounts of the studios have stressed the advantage of this position, with attendant opportunities for the observation of natural phenomena. They were 'built close to the seashore, looking upon the long Atlantic rollers foaming upon yellow sands – a rare opportunity for a sea painter to study wild weather and raging seas comfortably from his own windows'.[3]

Most importantly rents were low. It is a much-repeated myth that the reasons artists came to St Ives were for the landscape and the extraordinary light. These were certainly important factors, but far more important for many artists were pressing economic imperatives; it was cheap.[4]

It seems likely that Edward Simmons was the first artist to work at Porthmeor. Arriving in St Ives in early 1886, Simmons rented a loft overlooking Porthmeor Beach, installed a skylight, and worked there through the summer, together with three other artists. The American Howard Butler arrived a few weeks after and also secured a Porthmeor fish loft, cutting a window into the roof and whitewashing the interior. Butler stayed in St Ives until September 1887; when he returned in the mid-1890s he observed that a row of twenty-four fish lofts along Porthmeor had now been converted into studios.

From the early 1890s the studio complex was established, and from that point on it occupied a central position within the art colony in St Ives.[5] Many of the most important artists in the town worked here, including Julius Olsson, Algernon Talmage, Louis Grier, Alfred Hartley and Arthur Meade, as well as important visiting artists such as Emanuel Phillips Fox and Herbert Draper. Moffat Lindner, who had first visited St Ives with Philip Wilson Steer and Fred Brown, took a Porthmeor Studio, probably No.11, from 1899. Lindner was to play a key role in the future development of the studios. He purchased the freehold in 1929, thus ensuring that the complex could remain as artists' studios, available at reasonable rents, rather than be developed into holiday apartments. When in 1948 Linder was forced to sell the building due to increasing ill health, he agreed to a low price on the condition that the block was purchased for use as studios in perpetuity. A fundraising campaign by the Borlase Smart Memorial Fund, aided by a loan from the Arts Council, subsequently secured the studios.

Consequently the Borlase Smart Trust was formed to administer the studio complex, which it has done ever since.

Essentially the history of the studios can be divided into three phases. The first, up to 1949, is necessarily sketchy.[6] After 1949, when the studios began to be administered by the Trust, records started to be kept and it is possible to chart the changing occupancies with some accuracy. However, the picture is still far from clear, due to inconsistencies of numbering in reference to the individual studios and, more importantly, the practice of sub-letting, which was mostly carried out on an unofficial and ad hoc basis. The third significant phase begins with the opening of Tate St Ives in 1993, when Tate started to have a more active involvement with the studio complex, initiating projects and residencies. This phase will culminate with the refurbishment and development of the studios, creating a resource for St Ives and viable studio spaces for the twenty-first century.

This publication does not aim to offer a history of art in St Ives; rather it presents a (necessarily) partial history of the studios and examines their importance within the context of art in St Ives (and by implication British art) from 1880 to the present day. The place and meaning that both the studios and the art produced there occupies in the history of the art colony is explored, focusing on particular moments and on certain artists for whom the studios and their period of occupancy were of importance. Their work is examined to see if there is any connection between subject, style, technique and the spaces in which the paintings were made, and the locations of those spaces; by the beach, by the sea. The focus is entirely on painting, as the studios have been occupied almost exclusively by painters.[7]

A number of recent commentators have questioned the received view that the kind of painting made in St Ives in the post-war period

was largely defined by the surrounding landscape. Margaret Garlake
has argued that 'St Ives painting is heterodox and assimilative, by no
means exclusively concerned with the locality, despite the insistence of
numerous commentators that the place has, almost unaided, fostered
the development of a school of romantic painting'.[8] In his recent
monograph on Roger Hilton (who sub-let No.8 from Trevor Bell in
the late 1950s), Adrian Lewis proposes that 'the evocation of natural
phenomena within an abstract painterly style', which is typical of
modernist St Ives painting, was part of a wider cultural shift reflected not

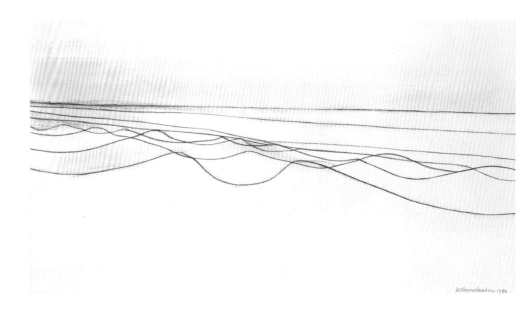

Wilhelmina Barns-Graham (1912–2004)
Eight Lines, Porthmeor
1986
Chalk on paper
34.5 × 62.7 cm
Tate
© Barns Graham Charitable Trust
Photo © Tate

only in Cornwall but in London, New York and elsewhere. He suggests that it was this 'rather than any geographical place, that created the context in which reference to the external world was licensed' in abstract painting.[9] Lewis goes on to stress that 'the locale of a painter is not what determines that artist to evoke associations at some level with that location. Places do not cause artistic change; nor do they provoke either the decision to allow suggestions of place or the specific way they are used.'[10] Whilst this is certainly true of Hilton – whose work of the period is concerned with abstract pictorial values, materials and the handling of paint, rather than notions of place – it is not completely true of all Hilton's contemporaries, or of the colony as a whole.

Garlake and Lewis are certainly correct in their assertions that the factors that contributed to the distinctive qualities of St Ives painting in the decades following the war were not simply derived from the surrounding landscape; the situation is far more complex than such a reading would imply. Nevertheless, reviewing the work made across the twentieth century at Porthmeor it is difficult to escape the conclusion that the location and the aspect of the studios had a powerful effect on many of the artists working there. Mel Gooding has recently suggested (apropos Wilhelmina Barns-Graham, who occupied No.1 for almost twenty years from the mid-1940s) that:

> St Ives and its environs seemed to provide perfect topographies to match an impulse to simplifying abstraction. The geometric angularities of stone architecture, the sweeping curves of the bays, the infinitely changing blues of sea and sky, bright morning light and the prismatic effulgence of sunsets, the wave line and overlap of incoming tidal currents across Porthmeor Bay, the irregularities of the rocky headlands and the green swell of the Island promontory against the sky and horizon: these contrasts

Sandra Blow (1925–2006)
Porthmeor
1996
Acrylic on canvas
259 × 260cm
Courtesy the estate of Sandra Blow
Photo © Bob Berry, St Ives

and their dynamics were for Barns-Graham then, and ever after, the definitive aspects of the scene. The deeper source of creative vision may remain inaccessible to analysis; it is what the artist makes of given circumstances, topographical and historical, transforming subject matter in an unprecedented manner, that indicates an original and distinctive view of the world.[11]

A number of artists who have worked in the studios, including Trevor Bell and Breon O'Casey, have confirmed that much of their work was a direct response to the specific conditions of the location; was indeed inspired by the sea view or the sea itself. More recently, *Porthmeor* 1996 (private collection), a resolutely abstract painting by Sandra Blow, seems nonetheless to evoke the light and space characteristic of the studios, the beach, the bay and the sea; a connection made explicit by its title.[12] Even when the subject is not specifically the beach or the sea it seems that these elements are woven into the work of the artists using the studios. The abstract painter Michael Seward Snow occupied No.8 from 1962 until 1968. His work apparently makes little reference to landscape, yet he wrote in 1964: 'I see my work as a sort of research into my surroundings.'[13] In 1985 David Lewis commented of the view from Barns-Graham's studio, No.1 Porthmeor: 'It has always seemed to me that Willie's Swiss Glacier series of paintings … majestic and sensuous experiences of whites, blues and greys, transparencies and opacities, were more paintings of that window than they were of ice and snow at Grindelwald'.[14]

Indeed, it is interesting to note how many of the artists who have worked in the studios have seen their work undergo radical change on arrival there. Again, it is simplistic to imply that this is attributable only to the location of the studios; many factors are at play. But certainly the very distinctive character of the studio spaces, their extraordinary location and unusual size are of central importance.

Algernon Talmage (1871–1939)
Evening at St Ives
Oil on canvas
40.6 × 45.7 cm
Courtesy of Messum's,
The Studio, Lords Wood, Marlow

2   Early Days

The major figure in the early history of the Porthmeor Studios is Julius Olsson. Born in London in 1864, Olsson worked for four years in the City office of a bank before deciding to become an artist. He arrived in St Ives in 1890 and quickly rose to prominence within the recently established art colony, remaining there until about 1911, after which he maintained strong connections with the town. Olsson achieved considerable success in England, exhibiting regularly at the Royal Academy in London; he was elected Associate of the Royal Academy (ARA) in 1914 and became a Royal Academician (RA) in 1920. He was also successful internationally, winning two Gold medals at the Paris Salon and twice being elected to the International Jury of the Carnegie Institute, Pittsburgh.

Olsson was the central figure of a group of established artists in St Ives that included, among others, Louis Grier, Algernon Talmage, Arthur Meade, Arnesby Brown, John Noble Barrow, Moffatt Lindner, and Millie Dow. It was these artists that brought the St Ives art colony to national attention and many of them, including Olsson, Talmage, Lindner and Meade, occupied Porthmeor Studios.

The artist and critic A.G. Folliott Stokes described Olsson as 'a big man with a big heart, painting his pictures with a big brush in a big studio', and for a time he certainly seems to have had an enormous studio at the heart of the Porthmeor complex.[1] When exactly he moved in is not clear but he was probably in occupancy in 1895 when he and Louis Grier opened a school of marine painting, which was run from the studio with classes being conducted on the St Ives beaches, including Porthmeor. It seems likely that Olsson's studio encompassed what were to become Nos.4, 5 and 6. Certainly a photograph of him in his studio taken circa 1900 shows him reclining next to the window of what is now No.6. The studio space is huge and open, and has two large sea-facing windows. This is the space now occupied by Nos.4 and 6, which have one window each. Later photographs of the St Ives Society of Artists exhibitions show the doorway between Nos.4 and 5, (now blocked up), as open, as shown on page 34. This would have made a vast space and was almost certainly the largest studio in St Ives at the time.[2]

Olsson was largely self-taught. He developed a method of working based on the close study of natural phenomena that was broadly in sympathy with concurrent developments in European painting, often characterised as *plein-airism*. His artistic credo was direct observation of nature and this entailed going out onto the land, whatever the weather conditions, and working in front of the motif. Borlase Smart later wrote that 'he believed in studying each bit of his subject mentally and intimately, assisted by quick colour notes. He got out of his studio and went straight to nature and this quickened his reactions, so that his pictures responded to the freshness of the open air.'[3] Crucially, however, while Olsson was a passionate advocate of working outdoors in order to experience and observe nature, a large part of his practice was carried out in the studio, working from memory and from notes and sketches.

Although Olsson painted some landscapes and mythological subjects, he focused almost exclusively on marine scenes and seascapes. These were often depicted at dusk or at night, in order to capture contrasts of light; the sinking sun, moonlight reflected across the water. Olsson's Porthmeor studio provided him with an excellent viewpoint from which to study the sea at all times and under every condition.

Olsson's subjects and his handling of paint and colour seem to be more closely aligned with those of French contemporaries such as Claude Monet than the more overtly socially engaged work of Jean-Francois Millet or Jules Bastien-Lepage, to whom many of the painters of Newlyn, turned for inspiration. Olsson's paintings are primarily about the quality of light, the evocation of space and form. The subject is sight itself; any human interest in the thing depicted is secondary. In Kenneth McConkey's apt formulation, Olsson's work is about 'seeing, rather than reflecting upon what is seen.'[4] This is the reason many of Olsson's seemingly empty images can appear strikingly modern to the contemporary eye.[5]

Although tangential to the history of the studios, it is worth briefly considering the distinctions between the kinds of art made in Newlyn and St Ives during this period, and whether or not the circumstances of location, and in particular the location of the studios, may have informed these differences.

The two art colonies were established at about the same time. Many of the artists at both St Ives and Newlyn had previously worked in the colonies at Concarneau, Pont Aven, Fontainbleau and Greuz, and were looking for locations in England where this experience might be repeated. Quite quickly, Newlyn became recognised for a particular and distinct kind of painting – broadly characterised as Naturalism or Social Realism – which was strongly identified with progressive French tendencies. The work of the Newlyn painters is exemplified by Realist genre scenes such as Stanhope Forbes's *Fish Sale on Newlyn Beach* 1884 (Plymouth Museum and Art Gallery) and Frank Bramley's *A Hopeless Dawn* 1888 (Tate), which found gradual acceptance at the Royal Academy. In St Ives, the artists were drawn towards the less socially engaged, more aesthetically orientated position of the New English Art Club. Realist paintings of social scenes were made in St Ives (by W.H.Y. Titcomb, for example), but the dominant tendency was towards pure landscape painting. On both sides of the Penwith peninsula *plein-air* painting was the dominant mode, but the products of St Ives were more in sympathy with the innovations of Impressionism – then becoming better known and understood – albeit filtered through an English tradition heavily indebted to Turner and Constable.

An early account of the two colonies by the artist and critic Norman Garstin offers concrete reasoning for the very different character of the art made in the two towns:

> The distance in mere miles between the two art colonies is insignificant; a moderately good walker finds it a pleasant afternoon's trudge over the breezy moor land, bright with gorse and furze, and ominously strewn with boulders and extinct mine chimneys, while the sea stretches away behind and before him … Newlyn looks East – there are no sands, the fringe of the

sea is not very alluring; and the sun soon sinks behind the hill on which the village lies, but this gives the figure-painter an admirable opportunity for placing his personages in shadow with a grey or glowing background of sea, hence many of the Newlyn motifs. St Ives, on the Northern coast, has a North-east to a North-western aspect; the sun comes gleaming over the water in the morning on one hand and sinks gleaming into it on the other hand in the evening; big waves come tumbling over white sands, and the foam is dyed in turns with all the colours of the spectrum; out of the windows of their foam-spattered studios the St Ives artists can watch the sea prinking itself in all the many tinted garments of the day and evening, and so they become impressionistic and sensuous in colour.[6]

Garstin's reading of the situation in the colony is a convincing explanation as to this difference and suggests that the very physical proximity of the studios in St Ives to the beach and the sea itself – that extraordinary view – was also a determining factor.

In 1910 Stokes described Olsson as 'our greatest sea painter'.[7] In a country with such a strong tradition of marine painting this was obviously intended as high praise. Yet Olsson's work represented a challenge to the orthodoxy of marine painting in late nineteenth-century Britain, in which the sea was generally presented either as a metaphor, or as a backdrop to a human drama being played out either on a boat or on the shore. As McConkey suggests: 'The sea is not neutral: it is the site for allegory, for fortune, fate and the hand of God. More than any other genre, marine and coastal scenes overtly addressed the natural virtues of an island race.'[8] In Olsson's paintings the sea is not symbolic, nor is it the setting for narrative. Olsson's focus is almost entirely on the play of light on water, and the rendering of space (often without perspective).

Where boats or other details do appear, they seem minor details in the composition. Olsson deliberately gave many of his paintings rather vague and prosaic titles such as *Cloudy Moonlight c.* 1925 (Doncaster Museum and Art Gallery) or *Cornish Coast c.* 1920 (Royal Academy, London) which describe the time of day or the weather conditions depicted, rather than directing the viewer to a poetic reading of the subject. Olsson also largely avoided identifying specific locations, perhaps to suggest that many of his paintings are not depictions of actual places, but rather an accumulation of responses to observed phenomena.

It is tempting to read Olsson's kind of painting, his seemingly empty compositions in which nature is reduced to its essentials – light and space – as a precursor of the kinds of art that dominated St Ives in the second half of the twentieth century. Whilst this would seem simplistic, it is certainly true that Olsson was a strong artistic personality and that his work was both successful and influential in the colony. It exemplified the major tendency within St Ives painting for the next fifty years, in clear contrast to the prevailing style in Newlyn.

Art historian Nina Lubbren has usefully employed sociologist Kevin Shield's conception of 'place-myths' as a way of exploring the development of artists' colonies in the late nineteenth century. The place-myth is 'the skein of expectations, hopes, stereotypes and associations attached to a place'. Through a process of 'over-simplification, stereotyping, labelling and activating prejudices, these conceptions crystallise into symbolic formations' or 'place-images' which collectively create the place-myth.[9] Olsson, with his powerful and distinctive work, his strident promotion of *plein-air* techniques, his public identification with St Ives (both through his art school and his exhibits at the annual Royal Academy exhibitions) and particularly his compelling public image – as written about in magazines and depicted in a series of evocative studio photographs – contributed

Julius Olsson (1864–1942)
Moonlit Shore
c1911
Oil on canvas
117.5 × 153.7 cm
© Tate

to the beginnings of a particular place-myth for St Ives. In the postwar period the arrival of Ben Nicholson, Wilhelmina Barns-Graham, Terry Frost, Patrick Heron and others at Porthmeor consolidated associations with painting-from-nature, and the identification of a St Ives 'style' or school with Porthmeor. In the 1990s, this way of thinking about St Ives was further reinforced by the creation of Tate St Ives.

At least five schools have been run from the Porthmeor Studios and, in addition, a number of artists based in the studios, including Frances Hodgkins and Marcella Smith, have offered private tuition there. The earliest of the schools was announced in the *St Ives Weekly Summary* in 1895:

> Two young artists, Mr Louis Grier and Mr Julius Olsson, are announcing the opening in St Ives, Cornwall, of a School of Landscape and Marine Painting. The main idea of this School is to give students an opportunity of studying out of door effects, and therefore the work of students will, weather permitting, be carried on actually in the open air, and will only be taken into the studio when atmospheric conditions render open air painting impossible.'[10]

Initially the school was run from Olsson and Grier's studios at Porthmeor. When Olsson rented the Harbour Studio in 1898 classes were probably conducted there too. The students would assemble at eight in the morning 'in the great studio … in time to see Olsson fold back the big doors above the beach. This created an opening the width of three or four fishing boats abreast. A metal bar was then dropped across the gap on which Olsson would lean when he relaxed with his pipe to study the sea and sky.'[11] Olsson would look at the students' work of the previous day and criticise it before sending them out onto the beach – whatever the weather – to work there until dusk. He was a hard taskmaster. Students were not allowed to sit at their easels but had to work standing up. Due to the often hostile weather they were encouraged to use heavy duty equipment so that it would not blow away.[12] They were encouraged to develop their powers of observation, speed of touch and visual memory: skills Olsson felt were essential for the study of nature and specifically the sea.

Olsson worked with Grier until c.1897 when he left and was replaced by Algernon Talmage. Talmage and Olsson then ran the school together until about 1901. By 1903 Olsson was described only as an 'honorable visitor' in publicity material, suggesting his decreasing involvement but also indicating the considerable cachet that his association produced. In 1907 Talmage was running the school, assisted by his wife Gertrude.

The school was very successful, and over the years the students included a number of artists who went on to become key figures in the colony, such as John Park and Borlase Smart. By attracting students to the town and promoting the *plein-air* techniques used by Olsson, Grier, Talmage and others, the school played an important role in the colony's early development and the particular kinds of painting practiced.

While Olsson may not have been based at Porthmeor for as long as has been previously assumed, he still emerges from this period as a key figure for the history of the studios.[13] His personality and reputation, his powerful paintings of the sea, his strong advocacy of a particular approach to landscape to his pupils, all contributed to the development of St Ives as a centre for landscape and marine painting. His connection with Porthmeor is reinforced by evocative photographs showing him in his vast, spare, studio, standing at a huge open window, palette in hand, as if seeking or awaiting inspiration from the extraordinary view before him.

St Ives Artists Society
Spring Exhibition,
Porthmeor Gallery
1934
© Tate

3   Between the Wars

Olsson's domination of the art scene in St Ives came to an end when he moved to London, soon after the purchase of *Moonlit Shore* by the Chantry Bequest for the Tate Gallery in 1911 and his election as ARA. Despite the presence in the town of a number of interesting artists, the period from the First to the Second World Wars has the feeling of an interlude. When Christopher Wood visited in1926 he carefully avoided 'the many painters painting picturesque views.'[1]

The New Zealander Frances Hodgkins had first visited St Ives in 1902. After time spent travelling in Europe and North Africa, and at home in New Zealand, she eventually arrived back in 1914 and was to remain there – with the exception of short periods spent in London – until October 1920. In St Ives Hodgkins hoped to make a living by teaching. For many artists, particularly those whose work was progressive and who could not therefore rely on sales or commissions, this was the only way to survive as a practicing artist. It was therefore crucial to her that the studio should be big enough to conduct classes in. For almost all of her time in St Ives she occupied No.7 in the Porthmeor Studios block, taking on 'a large empty studio next door' – probably No.8 – for her classes in the winter of 1915.

Hodgkins's letters to her friends and family offer a vivid account of St Ives during the war, her struggles to make ends meet, and her life in the studio. She arrived in late October 1914 and soon wrote to her mother Rachel that she was busy fixing up a studio: 'It is [a] huge barn that will do very nicely for a Class not pretty – but useful. It gives on a yellow sandy beach & at high tide the waves beat against the walls & sometimes the window – for this commodious loft – studio – pigsty – barn I pay £10 sterling a year.'[2]

At first Hodgkins lodged in the town and used the studio as working space. However, by June 1915, financial difficulties forced her to give up her rooms and move into the studio. Life was very difficult: her letters are filled with descriptions of the terrible weather, the freezing temperatures (blizzards were common during the winters) and the impossibility of keeping warm (a common dilemma for occupants of the studios even today): 'To warm myself I take sharp walks up & down the sands below my window – nobody but the seagulls & black masses of kelp looking like dead crocodiles in the deep dusk.'[3] She was amazed at the battering that the studio block took every winter. In November 1915 she wrote:

> We have just passed thru the fiercest storm for over 40 years. It began to blow about 10 at night – such a night. The studio rocked like a baby's cradle & at dawn looked like a drunkards home. The sky light blew in & of course floods of rain. About 4 o'c a fisherman came round and begged me to shelter in their house but I stuck it out, made a cup of cocoa & went to bed again… Tiles rained down in the courtyard & windows & chimneys crashed and banged. One man's studio close by was blown clean down and half out to sea…[4]

At this time the sand was banked high up against the sea-facing side of the building (a situation which would get steadily worse, eventually reaching crisis point in the early 1950s; see p.53). This meant that the sea would literally crash at the windows of the studios. In January 1915 she wrote: 'The weather was atrocious, one long blizzard. The

Frances Hodgkins (1869–1947)
**Loveday and Ann: Two Women
with a Basket of Flowers**
1915
Oil on canvas
67.3 × 67.3 cm
Tate

rain and sea came into my studio.'[5] A year later she reported: 'It is like a noisy cab rank below my windows – the shingles being hurled about by the high tides'.[6] It must have been very difficult to work in such conditions.

In St Ives Hodgkins began to experiment both stylistically and technically, exploring the innovations of Post-Impressionism, which she had seen in Paris during her travels. She quickly came to the conclusion that her work was more advanced than that of most of the artists in the colony: 'I find I am too modern for people down here & I am conscious of the cold eye of distrust & disapproval by the older member of St Ives. It is not an inspiring atmosphere tho I love it for many other things.' Despite this, one of the best things about the town, for her, was the studio: 'I will go a long way before I find another Studio like the one I have now.'[7]

The time spent in St Ives represented a transitional phase in Hodgkins' artistic development. Her pre-war work is Impressionist in manner, sensuous and light-filled, dominated by landscape and figures seen in sun-drenched landscape settings. She worked almost exclusively in watercolour, which she handled with great freedom and fluidity. In St Ives, however, the wartime restrictions on sketching out of doors meant that she was forced to focus on studio-based work such as figure studies and portraiture. She began to work in oils and – perhaps influenced by the wartime conditions – her works began to show greater austerity, gravity and stylisation, as can be seen in such group portraits as The Belgian Refugees c.1916 (Robert McDougall Art Gallery, Christchurch, New Zealand) and The Edwardians 1918 (Auckland City Art Gallery).

Her treatment of colour during this period was transformed, as can be seen in Loveday and Anne 1915 (Tate). In this painting of the daughters of a local fisherman, colour is freed from a strictly descriptive role and used to model form and to convey emotion, contributing to the conviction that Hodgkins has captured the atmosphere of easy familiarity between the two girls. The bold colouring and handling of paint strongly recall works by Bonnard and Vuillard.

In spite of her difficulties she found St Ives a good place to work. She had a fairly steady trickle of visiting students, as well as some locals.[8] Of great importance to her was the friendship of Moffat Lindner, whose portrait she painted in 1916. Lindner was open-minded enough to support artists working in more progressive ways than he, and for Hodgkins his encouragement and moral support were vital. He also helped in more concrete ways, commissioning the portrait and giving Hodgkins introductions and contacts in London.

Hodgkins later called this period her 'experimental years.' By the time she left St Ives in 1920 she had completely abandoned her earlier style and was committed to a more modern approach.

Two of Olsson's students, John Anthony Park and Borlase Smart, were to become key figures in the art colony between the wars, forming a bridge between Olsson's generation and the Modernists who arrived after the Second World War. They both, at times, worked from Porthmeor studios and their paintings represent a continuation of Olsson's principles.[9]

John Park first arrived in St Ives in 1899. Impressed by his natural talent, Olsson waived his tuition fees at the School. He became an important influence on Park, as did Grier and after 1900, Talmage. In 1905, on Olsson's advice, Park left St Ives for Paris, where he studied with Delacluse at the Academie Colarossi and was able to see works by the Impressionists, which had a lasting influence upon him. After this he travelled, spending time in Concarneau, Brittany, in 1911 and

John Anthony Park (1880–1960)
Morning Tide
1924
Oil on canvas
101.6 × 129.5 cm
Harris Museum & Art Gallery, Preston, UK

making occasional visits to St Ives. In 1923 he moved back to St Ives on a permanent basis, occupying a number of different studios, including No.10 Porthmeor from 1939 onwards. He exhibited regularly at the Royal Academy and at the Paris Salon in 1924 and 1934.

Despite its engagement with Impressionism, Park's work exemplifies an attitude to painting, and an approach to the subjects of St Ives – sea and coast – introduced by Olsson. He was a committed *plein-air* painter and for many years was seen regularly working in and around the town. He particularly favoured a shallow view across the harbour, with boats in the middle ground, which allowed him to capture the broken reflections of hulls, masts and colourful sails. Park's approach to such subjects is fundamentally Impressionist; colour is dissembled in order to capture the infinite variety of the play of light. His varied technique ranges from characteristically Impressionist 'dabs' of pure colour, to very fluid brushstrokes or the development of a dry, textured, scumbled surface, colour upon colour. On occasion his use of colour is extraordinarily vivid, going beyond an Impressionist concern with the accurate rendering of light to suggest a form of Post-Impressionism, as seen in the intensely green clouds in *Boats in St Ives Harbour* (private collection) or the hectic brushwork of *Morning Tide*1924 (Harris Museum & Art Gallery). It is this aspect of his work that led to the art historian David Brown's assessment that Park worked in 'a post-impressionist manner that was as near as St Ives got to the mainstream of modern art before [Ben] Nicholson's arrival in 1939'.[10]

Park's contemporary Borlase Smart studied with Olsson towards the end of his time in St Ives. After early success as an unofficial war artist – he exhibited drawings made while serving in France at Plymouth Art Gallery and then the Fine Art Society in London in 1917 – he returned to St Ives in 1919, where his 'boundless enthusiasm, his forthrightness and his helpfulness' meant that he was soon established as an important figure within the colony.[11] He was Honorary Secretary of the St Ives Society of Artists from 1930 and President in 1947. Smart moved in to No.1 Porthmeor in 1924, working there until 1944. He then moved to No.5, which he occupied until his death in 1947.

Smart was also a *plein-air* painter. He was particularly drawn to the craggy coastline of Penwith, painting many views down onto the sea from above, with steep cliffs and rocky outcrops in the fore and middle ground. He returned again and again to the sea as subject and his seascapes such as *Clear After Rain* c.1913 (St Ives Town Council) and *Ebb Tide on the Reef* 1943 (Swindon Museum and Art Gallery) are much indebted to Olsson, not only in their concentration upon the effects of light and atmosphere, but in their seemingly empty compositions and absence of symbolic content. In 1934 Smart published *The Technique of Seascape Painting*, which in its advocacy of *plein-air* techniques, boldness, and attention to form and movement, was essentially a primer in Olsson's artistic method and philosophy.[12]

With Leonard Fuller, who was to arrive in 1938 and found the St Ives School of Painting at No.11 Porthmeor, Park and Smart forged a connection with the old school in St Ives and the younger artists who arrived during or after the Second World War.[13] While Park was much respected by the younger artists, Smart actively encouraged links with them. For example, when Wilhelmina Barns-Graham arrived in the town in 1940 he befriended her and was able to arrange for her to sub-let No.3 from the marine painter George Bradshaw, who was then on active service. For Show Day in 1944 Smart invited Ben Nicholson to show work alongside his own in his Porthmeor studio.[14] This was Nicholson's first formal presentation of his work in the town.

Borlase Smart (1881–1947)
Ebb Tide on the Reef
Exh Royal Academy 1943
Oil on canvas
Swindon Museum and Art Gallery
Photo: Ben Cavanna

Sadly, Smart's efforts to reconcile traditional and modern were not appreciated by all. Barns-Graham later remembered him as 'rather a lone figure (in the St Ives Society of Artists) with his wider appreciation of art and searching spirit'.[15]

On 14 January 1927 the *St Ives Times* published a notice signed by Bradshaw, calling for a meeting to discuss the possibility of forming a society for artists in St Ives. In the same paper W.H. Truman contributed an article discussing the need to raise the quality of art in St Ives. At the meeting on 19 January it was decided to form a society. The founder members of the St Ives Society of Artists (SISA), which included both artists and lay members, included Moffat Lindner, Bradshaw, Bernard Leach, Park, Shearer Armstrong, Truman, F. Spenlove and Martin Cock. Lindner was elected the first President.[16] The Society's first exhibition opened at Lanham's Gallery in St Ives on 20 May 1927.

In spring 1928 the Society secured No.5 Porthmeor for use as a gallery. The first show there was opened by Olsson on 16 June 1928, and included work by St Ives artists and others associated with Cornwall, including Lindner, Olsson, Adrian Stokes, Stanhope Forbes, Lamorna Birch, Park, Bradshaw, Smart, Ernest Proctor, Dod Proctor, Alethea Garstin, Shearer Armstrong, Terence Cuneo and W. Arnold Foster. The gallery was extended into No.4 in 1932.

The Porthmeor Gallery was hugely important not only for the St Ives Society but for the art colony as a whole. It was not only a popular display space where many thousands of people (including the annual influx of summer visitors) could see the latest work by the artists of St Ives, but also provided the community of artists with a focus. The presence of the gallery reinforced the status of the studios and Porthmeor's position at the heart of the art colony in St Ives.

However, these changes coincided with a decline in the number of artists in the town and also available studio space, as tourism and the corresponding need for accommodation increased. By the 1930s St Ives was no longer recognised as an important centre for contemporary art, as it had been in the late nineteenth and early twentieth centuries when the Newlyn and St Ives colonies were at their peak and when large numbers of paintings from the towns were characteristically hung together at the annual Royal Academy exhibitions. Truman's article was symptomatic, to a large extent, of an art colony that had become complacent and conservative. Increased numbers of tourists meant increasing demand for unassuming scenic and marine paintings and many of the artists in the town were happy to provide. St Ives seemed, to a large extent, to have lost its distinctive artistic identity.

This was all to change after the war.

Ben Nicholson (1894–1982)
August 1956 (Val d'Orcia)
Oil, gesso and pencil on board
122 × 213.5 cm
© Angela Verren Taunt
Photo © Tate

4   After the War

In early February 1948 the hastily convened Borlase Smart Memorial Fund (Smart had died the previous year) issued a prospectus seeking funds to buy the Porthmeor Studios. The prospectus included a dire warning about the declining numbers of artists' studios in St Ives, and highlighted the importance of the Porthmeor block:

> This fund has been inaugurated in memory of Borlase Smart, ROI, RBC, who devoted his life to the art of painting and to the furtherance of Cornish Art, in particular that of the colony of St Ives. Because he knew so well the seriousness of the studio situation, it was his wish to procure for the St Ives Society of Artists, of which he was Honorary Secretary for many years, the block of thirteen studios known as the Porthmeor Studios.
>
> This, together with the object of furthering Cornish Art, is the primary purpose of establishing the fund.
>
> One can hardly exaggerate the seriousness of the present studio position in St Ives, the number of those available for the use of professional painters having dwindled from one hundred to thirty-eight, and, unless the Porthmeor block is secured for the artists by the Society, there is little doubt that the colony will fall apart and eventually cease as an art centre.[1]

At the age of ninety-six Moffat Lindner had decided to sell the studios.

He agreed to offer them to the St Ives Society of Artists for the reduced price of £6,000, on the condition that the studios were secured for the use of artists in perpetuity, and that the existing tenants be retained for as long as they wanted to stay. The Society immediately began to look at ways to raise the necessary funds.

On 12 February 1948 Philip James, Director of Art for the Arts Council of England, who had been sent a copy of the prospectus, wrote to David Cox, then Honorary Secretary of the SISA, requesting a meeting. By April it was agreed that the Arts Council would lend £4,500 to the Society, on mortgage terms, but with no time limit for repayment. Later, this was revised and the money was lent interest free.[2] By this time £1,740 had been raised and so funds were in place to proceed.[3]

The Borlase Smart Trust was established to manage the studios and their finances. Originally the Board of Trustees was to comprise representatives of the Arts Council, St Ives Society of Artists and a prominent art school, such as the Royal College of Art. This was later changed to the Director of Art of the Arts Council, the Director of the Tate Gallery and the Chairman of the St Ives Society (later the Honorary Secretary). However, this produced a potential conflict of interests; as P.B. Williams of the solicitors Bird & Bird pointed out to Philip James in September 1948: 'it is difficult, if not impossible, to find anyone locally in St Ives who might not at the same time require to become a tenant of one of the studios who could be appointed as Trustee for the St Ives Society'.[4] This was eventually resolved by substituting the St Ives Society representative for a local Trustee who for many years was drawn from the land agency Lanhams. In more recent years the Board of Trustees has expanded to include the Directors of Tate St Ives and the Newlyn Art Gallery and locally based artists and writers.

The studios were formally taken over by the Trustees in March 1949. A press statement was issued the following month with the headline 'Arts Council Loan Saves St Ives Studios'. The tenants at this time were Wilhelmina Barns-Graham (No.1), Agnes Drey (No.2), Commander George Bradshaw (No.3), Leonard Richmond (No.4), David Cox (No.5), Frances Ewan (Nos.6 and 7, using one as living accommodation), Lucy Walsh (No.8), Alixe-Jean Shearer Armstrong (No.9), Hyman Segal (No.10) and Leonard Fuller (No.11). There were no contracts; all except Fuller had only informal verbal agreements with Lindner. The Trust immediately started to address this problem but the process of formalising tenancies and getting contracts in place for all the tenants was to take many years.

The Borlase Smart Trust has continued to administer the studio complex since 1949. The Trust's aims remain fundamentally the same as those outlined in the initial fundraising prospectus, albeit with a slightly wider remit. As well as managing the studios it also undertakes: 'The promotion of the highest standards of painting, sculpture, teaching, woodcutting and other graphic arts in St Ives in the County of Cornwall for the purpose of increasing public knowledge and appreciation of said arts'. [5]

The archive at the Arts Council offers an insight into the workings of the Trust, particularly in the early years. One surprising revelation is to see how few applicants there often were for vacant studios. It is possible that this was because a notion became entrenched quite quickly that the Arts Council was only likely to look favourably upon applications from artists with modernist tendencies. What is certain is that there was frequently a distinct lack of publicity about the availability of the studios and the application process. In December 1957, when Frances Ewan finally decided to vacate Nos.6 and 7, thus freeing up two studios, there were just five artists on the waiting list: Sandra Blow,

Marion Hocken, Roger Hilton, Alan Lowndes and Patrick Oliver. After the vacancies were advertised locally, Blow, Hilton and Hocken did not renew their applications and there were only three new applicants: Gwen Leitch, E. Boyle Mitchell and Cyril Milton. It was, in Philip James's word, 'disappointing'. Advertisements in London-based arts magazines produced only a single further application, from Bob Law. In the event the studio was offered to Gwen Leitch and Ewan decided to retain No.6, which she was able to do under the terms of her agreement with Lindner, much to the frustration of James and John Rothenstein, then Director of the Tate Gallery.

Applicants were considered in light of 'financial status and volume of need' as well as whether or not they were making 'work of a sufficient standard to warrant a serious consideration', although in the event the decision often relied more on 'volume of need' than the quality of the work.[6] Often the work of applicants was unknown to the Trustees, who were based in London and visited the the town infrequently, and so Gerald Cock of Lanhams and his successors were called upon to give their opinion. The support of artists such as Ben Nicholson and Patrick Heron, both of whom wrote a number of letters of recommendation over the years, was often crucial to the deliberations. In 1951, for example, Nicholson wrote in support of Frost, who was not known to James: 'he is about the most promising of all the painters here (and is at present working in a small back bedroom where he is constantly disturbed) – just as promising even I think as Lanyon + has had a v hard time trying both to get down to his painting + to make ends meet.'[7] Frost was subsequently offered No.4, thus becoming Nicholson's neighbour.

Very soon after the Trust took over and began to install new tenants there were accusations that the Arts Council was trying to promote a particular kind of art, despite the fact that the Trust did in fact

Wilhelmina Barns-Graham (1912–2004)
Studio Interior (Red Stool)
1945
Oil on canvas
46 × 61 cm
© Barns-Graham Charitable Trust

manage to maintain a remarkable balance between traditionalists and modernists in the studios. Nicholson was the first new tenant and at the time he moved in was a singular presence in a stronghold of conservatism; although this quite quickly changed with Wilhelmina Barns-Graham's moves towards abstraction around 1950 and the arrival of Frost in 1951.

Another matter of dispute which attracted angry letters from observers was the question of artists not making full use of their studios; either through being away and letting them sit empty, or sub-letting. Trevor Bell, for example, occupied No.8 for five years from 1957 to 1962 but was absent at various times on an Italian Government Scholarship and as Gregory Fellow of Painting in Leeds. During this period he sub-let to Roger Hilton for a year. Michael Snow, Karl Weschke and Anthony Benjamin may also have used the studio for shorter periods.

In 1962 the Trust moved to rationalise lettings, proposing to ask tenants to surrender their studios if not making use of them. It was eventually formalised that the minimum required occupation was eight months per annum. This was followed by letters to Bell, Barns-Graham (who was spending much time in Scotland), William Redgrave (who also had a Piazza Studio) and Ewan (who occupied two studios, living in one, but was no longer active as an artist) asking them to voluntarily give up their tenancies. By August 1962 all four tenants had agreed to leave. Subsequently No.1 was offered to Patrick Dolan (who waited so long for Barns-Graham to vacate that in 1963, when Frost also left, he moved into No.4, leaving Roy Conn to eventually take on No.1), No.3 to Alan Lowndes, No.6 to Cedric Rogers and No.8 to Michael Snow.

Periodically, concern was voiced about the need to provide studio space for younger artists. There was also an ongoing discussion about limiting the duration of the tenancies to ensure a changing population of artists. In the event, nothing was formalised and a number of artists were to remain for extremely lengthy periods. Hyman Segal was without doubt the longest resident, occupying No.10 for fifty-six years. Conn has been in No.1 for forty-two years, since 1963, and Heron was in No.5 for forty-one years. At the time of writing both Bob Crossley and Bryan Pearce have been resident for thirty-three years. Tony O'Malley was in No.4 for twenty-seven years (he had previously been in No.6 and had worked in other studios, such as No.3, on an unofficial basis).

The correspondence between the local Trustees and the Trustees in London at the Tate and Arts Council is a continual litany of small disasters: collapsing stoves, leaking roofs, blocked gutters, faulty electricity and so on. While Nicholson was unconcerned by the conditions of the studios when he moved into No.5 in 1949 – being so pleased with the amount of space he had – they were in fact little better, and if anything worse, than they had been when Frances Hodgkins was in residence and the sea regularly came into the studio through the windows. Over the years the Trustees have fought a running battle with deteriorating buildings but have been unable to do much more than make temporary repairs.

One particular problem throughout the first half of the century was the build up of sand from the beach against the sea-facing side of the buildings. By the early 1950s this had become so bad that some of the studio windows were almost completely obscured. A severe gale in January 1952 brought things to crisis point. Lucy Walsh wrote to Philip James to complain that there was almost no light in No.8 as sand almost completely blocked the window; the studio had become 'like a dungeon'.[8] Gerald Cock went to investigate and reported to Philip James:

> The position has worsened considerably, and the weight of the sand against the window of the studio occupied by Commander Bradshaw has resulted in the window collapsing into the studio bringing with it several tons of sand.[9]

The sand menace was caused by the tides and currents and affected all the buildings along Downalong. The debate about how to address it went on for some time, with the first efforts to shift the sand being made in 1944, and the Council reluctant to take responsibility due to the considerable expenditure required. However, eventually, in 1952 two bulldozers moved 40,000 tons of sand and the problem was abated.

The sand menace was a dramatic example of how a building on the beach, exposed to the Atlantic, might be affected by the elements. The Porthmeor studios have gradually been deteriorating for the past century, and conditions have remained problematic. In summer they are airy and light-filled, and for many of the artists the biggest problem to contend with has been the distractions of the beach. But in winter the lack of insulation and the exposure to the Atlantic means they are cold and damp. Nicholson habitually drew a ring around the drips from leaks in the ceiling of No.5, so that he wouldn't unwittingly position a painting where it might be damaged.

More recently, in 1984, Karl Weschke moved into No.9 and found it incredibly cold, so much so as to make it impossible to work there for long periods. He described how he would arrive in the morning and light the stove and then leave, only returning to the studio later in the day when some heat had built up. However, Weschke was forced to move in 1993 not because of the cold but because of the noise of the other tenants. No.9 is one of the few studios to have another directly above and the noise, particularly of people walking about, drove him to distraction. William Redgrave also cited this as reason for moving from No.12 to No.3 in 1958.

The walls between the studios are very thin and so noise has always been a potential problem. The Trust's tenancy agreements had attempted to address this issue right from the beginning, for example banning the use of radios in the studios. However, Nicholson protested vociferously claiming that he used a radio to help him concentrate when working, and the rule was amended.

*

At an extraordinary General Meeting of the St Ives Society in February 1949, David Cox, who was then Honorary Secretary, resigned over the selection process for the Society exhibitions. Shortly after, he gave up his Porthmeor Studio and the Trust was faced with the task of finding its first tenant.

In May Ben Nicholson wrote to Philip James from the house in Carbis Bay that he shared with Barbara Hepworth and their children:

> I have been unsuccessful ever since I came to this house in obtaining a studio in St Ives & I am forced to work in the small converted bedroom … this imposes a very definite limit on the size of painting I can make, & also I find it increasingly difficult during the "holidays" *to work at all* with a houseful of children.[10]

He wrote again a few days later:

> I forgot to mention in support of my application that I have a commission to design two panels for Howard Robinson for a

New Zealand ship & that they are much too large for me to tackle in this house. They will not in fact even go into my studio.

On my last attempt to secure a big studio in St Ives, when Borlase Smart was helping me, I nearly succeeded… when the block of which it was a part was purchased by a local 'reactionary' artist and the studio I'd applied for was let instead I was told, to some woman who paints very very small watercolours[11]

Nicholson moved into No.5 at the beginning of July, writing to James on 3 July to thank him. Nicholson had arrived in Cornwall in 1939, escaping the Blitz. He was eventually to stay for nineteen years. He had been in St Ives before, most famously in 1928 when he and Christopher Wood 'discovered' Alfred Wallis. In the intervening years, with works such as the white reliefs of the 1930s, he had established a reputation as one of the leading avant-garde artists in Europe. However, his work of the war years shows a degree of retrenchment, a return to earlier figurative modes perhaps prompted by both by his own situation and changing tastes and demand for art in a time of conflict and after.

The invitation to work in No.5 came at an important moment. Nicholson soon made himself at home there and began to work with renewed vigour. He hung a hammock in the studio and when Patrick Heron asked him whether he ever used it he replied: 'No, but just looking at it makes me feel as though I am resting.'[12] He did not mind that the studio was cold and that the roof leaked; he was exhilarated by the space. He wrote to Philip James in November 1949:

**5 Porthmeor Studios, St Ives,
(with part of Ben Nicholson's
Festival of Britain Mural in background)**
1949
© Tate

I have been greatly enjoying working in my large St Ives
AC Studio – the light and scale are both very fine & these
reasonable, normal conditions should have a considerable
effect on the work after 10 years of abnormal conditions – I
have several large still lifes on the go, one of which I've just
completed & it is looking rather exciting.[13]

The most immediate affect that the new studio had on Nicholson's work was an increase in scale. After years of working in cramped spaces it was 'like being able to breathe deeply again to be able to work on this scale – to walk about and painting at arm's length'.[14] In addition to the panels for the SS Rangitane, which were each almost two metres high, Nicholson soon completed a number of paintings on a scale bigger than anything he had done since the late 1930s. And in addition to large-scale easel paintings he was also now able to accept commissions for murals. In 1950 he was working on a three-panel mural over six metres across for the Festival of Britain and in 1952 he accepted a commission to produce a mural for the Time Life building in London.

In November 1949 Nicholson sent James photographs of recently completed works in the studio:

> The still life is a very recent work & is what I am really interested in at the moment as I like the more elaborate forms and organisation which emerge from the still life theme as well as the tension between a certain naturalistic illusion and abstraction.[15]

At Porthmeor Nicholson addressed the still-life theme, using it for an exploration of tension between 'naturalistic illusion and abstraction' that was to be his main preoccupation of the 1950s. These works are indebted to Cubism but are not volumetric; space is seen in terms of overlapping planes rather than solids. Compositions are articulated by taught linear drawing intertwined with washes of colour creating a synthesis of ground and motif. Interestingly, the colours often introduce landscape associations.

**Ben Nicholson in
5 Porthmeor Studios, St Ives,
with *1953 February (Contrapuntal)***
c1953
© Tate

It is worth noting that Nicholson occupied what was then the only
studio at Porthmeor that had no sea view. The single window from No.5
looks out onto the courtyard at the centre of the studio complex and
Nicholson blocked this in, in order to maximise the top light. In one
sense his work reflected these confined circumstances, being apparently
hermetic, locked into a repertoire of interior spaces and forms; bottles,
vases, goblets and cups arranged on tables. For the nine years that

he was to occupy No.5 Nicholson was to paint little else but table-top still-life compositions which were, however, highly abstracted and open to multiple readings. Despite the enclosed space in which they were made many of them are extraordinarily expansive and, paradoxically, do suggest a connection to landscape in the form of what Peter Khoroche has characterised as 'landscape memories'.[16] Nicholson acknowledged that there were interconnections between the two subjects. He said: 'My "still life" paintings are closely identified with landscape, more closely than are my landscapes which perhaps relate more to "still life".'[17] He wrote to Helen Sutherland: 'These still lifes, so-called, always turn out to be landscape for me.'[18]

June 4 – 52 (tableform) 1952 (Albright-Knox Art Gallery, Buffalo) seems to evoke the beach and seascape lying beyond the walls of the studio. There is a definite suggestion of a landscape form – a headland or the rolling forms of a ridge of hills – wrapping around the top edge of the still-life group and the possibility of a horizon line dividing blue sea and darker sky just below the top edge of the painting. The colours certainly evoke the Cornish coast and specifically Porthmeor beach and its setting: golden sand, pale blue sea, the dull green of heath and the blue grey of cliffs. The table top itself is fragmented into a series of shifting planes; the image composed of a series of sinuous interlocking lines, seemingly drawn tight around objects that they suggest rather than describe, and freely shifting planes of colour which move both forward and backwards in front and behind each other. Rather than evoking a still-life group on a windowsill, as some of Nicholson's earlier works do, here the imagery is fluid and the elements are inseparable. In 1952 Patrick Heron wrote of these works:

> The still life paintings are impregnated with qualities of light, texture and colour which convey one at once to St Ives. The

over-clean 'washedness' of the cool colours and smooth neat textures are qualities very precisely related to that rain-washed Atlantic-blown town. And the multiplicity of pale greys, off whites, pale blues, purples and yellows all have a valid basis in the white ocean-reflected light which almost bleaches things in its diffuse radiance.[19]

The 1950s were a very successful period for Nicholson and these new still-life abstractions were widely recognised as some of his finest works. By the end of the decade he was beginning to achieve in Britain the kind of recognition and critical acclaim that he had for some time enjoyed internationally. In 1954–5 he showed in the British Pavilion at the Venice Biennale and the exhibition subsequently toured to Amsterdam, Paris, Brussels and Zurich. This was followed by a major retrospective at the Tate Gallery in 1955. In addition Nicholson was awarded the prestigious Pittsburgh International award in 1952 and the first Guggenheim Painting Award in 1957.[20]

Nicholson was active in the life of the studio complex. He followed the selection process for tenants closely, often intervening, usually, but not always, in support of artists pursuing abstraction. Of his fellow tenants he was probably closest to Frost and Barns-Graham, both of whom he regularly invited to No.5 to discuss his work. Frost remembered that he kept cork-tipped Craven A cigarettes and sherry in the studio which he would offer in return for a critique.

When he left St Ives for Switzerland in 1958 Nicholson tried to secure an appropriate succession. He wrote to Philip James to argue that as the studio was suited to 'especially large scale work' it should go to someone who can 'really use it to advantage'.[21] He recommended that it be given to either Heron or Frost.

Trevor Bell (b1930)
Overcast
1961
Oil on canvas
61 × 61 cm
Tate
© the Artist

5   Abstraction and Figuration

Patrick Heron wrote to apply for Nicholson's studio from Eagles Nest, his house above Zennor, in June 1958. He stressed his need for space, but also light:

> It may seem odd, when I say I haven't enough space to paint my new large canvases up here at Eagles Nest! But my room here has less than half the floor area of Ben's No.5 Porthmeor – and is only a third the height. This studio here is in fact a Victorian dining room – large, as a dining room: small as a studio. The light here is purely *horizontal* – Ben's would be a godsend both for its overhead neutral light and its superb, quiet *space!*[1]

By the end of the month he had been offered the studio. At this time Peter Lanyon was sourcing studios for the American painters Robert Motherwell, Helen Frankenthaler and Sam Francis, who were intending to visit St Ives in the summer. Frankenthaler was to sub-let No.3 from William Redgrave and Lanyon hoped that Motherwell might use No.5 in July and August. Heron's response was that he would be happy for Motherwell to use the studio in August and September but that he was desperate to make some new large paintings and that he wanted to begin in the studio in July. He wrote to Philip James: 'I could, of course, offer Motherwell or Sam Francis a v large bedroom up here [at Eagles Nest] to work in!'[2]

In fact Heron did not start in the studio until August. His unwillingness to allow Motherwell to use the studio – which contributed to the failure of Lanyon's project and the intriguing possibility of three of the most prominent American artists of the period visiting St Ives to work – may have been to do with antagonism between him and Lanyon, but is more likely to do with the fact that at this time he was in the process of revising his opinion of the American painters, whose work he had previously supported. He had praised their work in print in 1956 but in May 1958 wrote that he missed in their output the 'sensuous subtlety of tone colour, a subtle asymmetry of shape, a varied tempo of working,' concluding that 'it is a terribly cramping thing, to be bound by a rigid concept of what *freedom* should look like in a painting'.[3]

Heron's move into No.5 came at a crucial stage in his development. His groundbreaking stripe paintings of 1957–8 had been poorly received when shown at the Redfern Gallery in March 1958, and indeed the gallery had closed the exhibition early. This, and his reassessment of the Americans, may have been catalysts for a renewed commitment to his own work and focused exploration of the pictorial possibilities of colour.[4] That summer he left the Redfern and joined Waddington's and in August 1958, just as he was starting to work in No.5, he resigned as London correspondent for the New York-based *Arts* magazine, resolving 'never again to write criticism'.[5]

Heron responded to his new studio by immediately producing a group of major works. These broke with the predominantly upright format of his recent paintings and were almost all landscape in shape. They also rejected the vertical register of recent works, which had been articulated either by the short vertical brushstrokes of the garden paintings or the tall stacks of horizontal strata-like brushstrokes arranged up tall, thin canvases, which was the dominant mode of the stripe paintings.

In new works such as *Brown Ground (with Soft Red and Green): August*

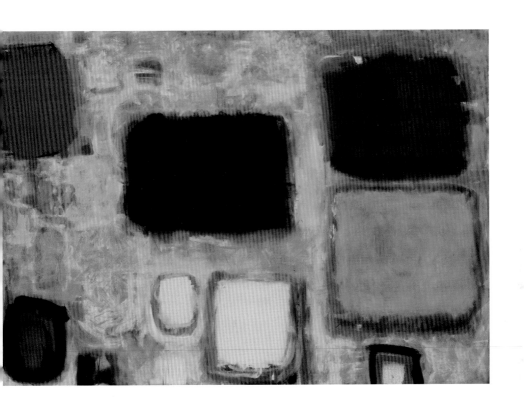

Patrick Heron (1920–1999)
Yellow Painting: October 1958 May/June 1959
1958–9
Oil on canvas
152 × 213 cm
Tate
© Estate of Patrick Heron
All Rights Reserved, DACS 2006

1958 – July 1959 (Tate) and *Yellow Painting: October 1958 – May/June 1959* (Tate) the stripes were broken and massed into 'lozenges'; floating rectangles, circles and ovoid forms which appeared to be spontaneous in conception and execution. These paintings were seemingly free of representational content; Heron had realised that even the stripe paintings could be read as distillations of landscape with ground, horizon and sky. Moreover they were generous in scale, being the biggest paintings Heron had yet made. They were celebratory of colour and were definitely, albeit indirectly, a response to the space and light of the new studio.

The complexity of texture and colour in works such as *Grey and Yellow (with Circle): October 1958 – February 1959* (private collection), *Blue Painting: November – December 1958* (private collection) and *Ragged Squares – Tall Painting: December 1958* (private collection), was also new to Heron's work, and derived in large part from his deployment of successive layers of over-painting. This was enabled by the studio space. Photographs of Heron's studio characteristically show the walls filled with a number of paintings in various stages of completion.[6] The space of the studio allowed Heron to work on a series of paintings simultaneously, as a group, over time. Seemingly spontaneous adjustments to the works (they are rich in *pentimenti,* the ghosts of successive revisions) could therefore be deeply considered. This contrasted with the 'one shot' approach of the earlier garden paintings and stripes. The generosity of space of the studio thus allowed him to establish a broad working method which he adhered to, more or less, for the rest of his life. Rather than working on individual paintings he would characteristically create a new body of work, usually for a specific exhibition.

Heron's use of the studio differed from usual practice in another way – he did not store work there. It was space for new work – work in progress

– and new work only. While Eagles Nest was hung with paintings from all periods of his career and thus formed a kind of visual archive for the artist, the Porthmeor studio was a work space, and for looking forward rather than back.[7]

Heron's new paintings produced a critical breakthrough. The following year he was awarded the Grand Prize by an international jury at the John Moores Painting Exhibition 1959 for *Black Painting – Red, Brown, Olive: July 1959* (Walker Art Gallery, Liverpool). Soon after, in 1960, he had his first solo show at Waddington's and his first show in New York, at the Bertha Shaefer Gallery.

One of the key ways in which Heron responded to No.5 was by increasing the size of his paintings. He had looked long and hard at the Americans – Pollock, Rothko, Kline, Motherwell, Still – and now had the opportunity to make work of comparable scale to them. Indeed, Heron was one of the only artists in St Ives to make paintings on anything like the scale of the Americans, and the Porthmeor space was undoubtedly a decisive factor in enabling this. However, while Heron's Porthmeor works of the late 1950s and early 1960s were big it was not until the late 1960s and 1970s that he began to make work on a very large scale, creating monumental canvases such as *Cadmium with Violet, Scarlet, Emerald, Lemon and Venetian 1969* (Tate) and *Big Cobalt Violet: May 1972* (private collection) and *March – April 1975* (private collection) – all over four metres across – which completely fill the spectator's field of vision creating an extraordinary immersive experience of colour. It is difficult to imagine any other space in St Ives in which such paintings could have been made.

*

The 1950s and 1960s saw the development of a wide-ranging pluralism in the visual arts in Britain, encompassing realism, abstraction (including both constructionist and gestural tendencies) and the nascent Pop Art movement. Divisions between representation and abstraction were reflected by the tenants of the studios, who in the early 1960s included abstract painters such as Heron, Frost, Barns-Graham, Trevor Bell, Roy Conn, Douglas Portway and Patrick Dolan, and figurative artists such as William Redgrave, John Barclay, Alixe Shearer-Armstrong, Hyman Segal and Alan Lowndes. Nonetheless, with Heron's success at the John Moores Exhibition in 1959 (when Roger Hilton was also a prizewinner) and the award of the Painting Prize at the Paris Biennale to Trevor Bell in the same year (these coming so soon after Nicholson's Tate Gallery retrospective and his Guggenheim Painting Prize) it was clear that abstraction was in the ascendant. By the end of the 1950s St Ives was strongly associated with a 'school' of abstract painting, albeit one characterised by its connections to landscape painting. In 1954 Lawrence Alloway sarcastically suggested that 'in St Ives they combine non-figurative theory with the practice of abstraction because the landscape is so nice nobody can quite bring themselves to leave it out of their art'.[8]

Given this context it is therefore surprising that in 1959 Francis Bacon chose St Ives to prepare for his first solo show with Marlborough Fine Art the following year.

Bacon arrived in St Ives in September 1959. He already knew a number of artists in the town, including Dolan and Redgrave, and when the latter bumped into him in the Sloop Inn and learnt that he was looking for a studio for six months he immediately offered him the use of No.3 Porthmeor, which was then being used as a venue for St Peter's Loft, the art school that he ran with Lanyon.[9] Bacon's tenancy would solve the problem of the lean winter months. Impressed by the space, Bacon immediately offered six months' rent, £38, in advance. Both Weschke and Law had been hoping to take the studio for the winter, but Redgrave reasoned that if he gave it to either of them he would have no reasonable expectation of reimbursement. In addition, for Redgrave the opportunity to have Bacon, the most important British figurative artist to have emerged since the war in St Ives, was too good to resist. Lanyon happily agreed to the scheme on the basis that Bacon loathed Heron, who would be his near neighbour at the studio. In fact, Bacon and his companion Ronald Belton eventually spent a very pleasant Christmas Day 1959 at Eagles Nest with Heron and his family.

Bacon's reasons for the temporary move to St Ives are unknown. Michael Peppiat has suggested that it was like 'a deliberate act of penance'.[10] The most likely explanation is that he wanted an opportunity to concentrate on his work without distractions, although it is possible that he was curious about recent artistic developments in the town. In the aftermath of his turbulent relationship with Peter Lacey he had left his dealer of the past decade, Erica Brausen, and joined Harry Fischer's Marlborough Fine Art. His new gallery had reportedly paid off extensive gambling debts and was now also paying him a substantial retainer. His first show for them was scheduled for March 1960 and he needed to produce a new body of work for it. It has been suggested that the St Ives sojourn was set up by Marlborough in order to get Bacon away from the distractions of London but there is no evidence to back this up. The fact that on his arrival Bacon was actively seeking a studio seems to suggest that nothing had been arranged in advance.

Bacon moved down to St Ives at the beginning of October, accompanied by Ronald Belton, and took up lodgings in a flat at 1 Seagull House, overlooking the harbour. On 19 October he wrote to Harry Fischer to say he had been 'lucky enough to find a wonderful studio' and he would let him know when there was work to see.[11] He told Redgrave that he was expecting a visit from Fischer and Helen Lessore in early December (which, it seems, did not come about) and started to work. He kept his characteristic hours – rising early and painting until lunch time – and Belton was allowed to use the studio in the afternoon.

Bacon mixed with the St Ives artists, drinking with them in the Sloop, the Castle and other pubs in the town and nearby. His clashes with abstract painters and sculptors are vividly described by Redgrave in his journal. For example, a meeting with Hilton:

> A carefully chosen insult from Roger. I have always wanted to meet you because I think you are the only non abstract painter worth consideration although of course you are not a painter you don't know the first thing about painting. Good said Francis – I think my work is perfectly horrible – now we can get together – you teach me how to paint and I'll lend you my genius.[12]

Bacon's views on abstraction, which he regarded as 'decoration', were well known. Redgrave noted of his encounters with artists such as Bryan Wall, Anthony Benjamin and Hilton that 'being new here and detached… he could lash them to his heart's content'. This was all fantastic stuff for Redgrave, who as a figurative artist felt increasingly marginalised by the growing success of the abstract painters in St Ives.

Bacon's stay was mostly uneventful. There were drinking sessions and late-night discussions. Belton got into trouble for thievery and one point after an argument with some locals outside the Sloop he punched Bacon in the face, knocking out a tooth. At the beginning of December Bacon sent five completed paintings up to London. In early January he announced he would have to leave. Any work he did after this time

Francis Bacon (1909–1992)
Lying Figure
1959
Oil on canvas
198 x 141.5 cm
Private collection, USA,
courtesy Faggionato Fine Art, London and New York

would not be dry enough to travel to London for the show and in any case he could not find a good dentist to replace the missing tooth.

Towards the end of Bacon's stay Redgrave visited No.3. He saw a dozen large stretchers out of which the canvas had been cut and two canvases with portrait heads – one finished, one unfinished – on easels. A group of canvases were stacked for transport: 'only one painted on – some arbitrary abstract rectangles – a black one in the middle on which is painted a male nude that is so lacking in any kind of beauty or dignity positively disgusting. *Positively* and that being the important thing – all the canons retreat like schoolmarms from a lunatic asylum.'[13] This work was almost certainly *Lying Figure* 1959 (private collection).

There were also a number of portrait studies. Bacon's female portraits from St Ives have usually been identified as Redgrave's wife Mary (known as 'Boots') but it seems odd, if Bacon had painted her, that Redgrave did not mention it in his journal. Instead he writes that Belton identified three of the heads as being of Muriel Belcher and that the best one looked like 'a tinted corpse'.[14] It may be that Bacon started three portraits of Belcher in St Ives, completing one, but that on his return to London, and with reworking, the remaining two were metamorphosed into representations of Mary Redgrave from memory. This often happened to Bacon's portraits. David Sylvester described sitting for a portrait in 1953 that in his absence was gradually transformed into a pope after Velásquez.

Bacon left in January and Belton stayed on a few extra days to sort out the studio and burn the rejected pictures.[15] No.3 Porthmeor was left in a state of chaos. Redgrave noted: 'Francis used anything for mixing paint dishes bowls pans chairs and all four of the small tables caked with paint still wet.'[16]

Bacon's stay in St Ives was brief. He worked hard while he was there but destroyed almost all he had done. Ronald Alley's *Catalogue Raisonné*, with which Bacon collaborated, lists just six paintings made in St Ives.[17] However, from Redgrave's account it is clear that there were a number of unfinished canvases that were shipped up to London, and Bacon may have completed these in his Battersea studio. Certainly works such as *Walking Figure* 1960 (Dallas Museum of Contemporary Arts), which Alley suggests was painted in London between Bacon's return and the show, imply a direct continuity with the St Ives pieces. Alley lists fifteen canvasses completed after Bacon's return to London and the opening of his show in March 1960. This implies a work rate of almost a picture every two days and, given that Bacon was a slow painter, seems extremely unlikely.

Bacon's stay in St Ives came in the middle of a five-year period of reassessment and experimentation which was bookended by the van Gogh series in 1957 that introduced a heightened palette, and the Tate Gallery retrospective of 1962 for which he painted the first of his great, mature triptychs, *Three Studies for a Crucifixion* 1962 (Guggenheim Museum, New York). While David Sylvester has suggested that in this period Bacon was, to a certain extent, 'lost' (singling out the surviving portrait of *Miss Muriel Belcher* 1959 (private collection) painted in St Ives as the finest work of this period), it was actually a period of crucial importance for Bacon's development. His paintings of this period are characterised by strongly coloured, uninflected backgrounds, often in strong greens and blues, against which figures or heads are positioned. While it is difficult to discern the direct influence of the work he might have seen in St Ives – despite his assertion that he 'looked at everything' – the possible influence of the show of American painting at the Tate in 1958, and in particular Rothko and Newman, has been much commented on. However, a work such as *Lying Figure* 1960 (Estate of Francis Bacon)[18] painted shortly after his stay in St Ives, suggests not only that Bacon had been looking at Rothko but perhaps Heron too. The bands of colour that form a setting for the figure strongly recall works such as *Red Layers (with Blue and Yellow): 14 December 1957* (private collection) or *Cadmium Scarlet: January 1958* (private collection), that Bacon may well have seen at Eagles Nest. Bacon's work of this period also makes use of flatness or extremely shallow pictorial space; values which Heron was assiduous in promoting. Gone are the 'spaceframes' which in his earlier works position the figures within a perspectival opening. Instead his figures are pressed, squashed even, like smears of paint, between the flat, unmodulated backgrounds and the glass that Bacon habitually framed them behind.

If St Ives had little effect on Bacon, was the reverse true? Certainly his visit there was of talismanic importance to figurative artists such as Redgrave.

One artist who did respond to the contact with Bacon was Karl Weschke. They met in the Sloop and quickly became friendly (the friendship continued in London, Bacon proposing Weschke for membership of the Colony Room), paying visits to each other's studios, although Weschke remembered that, initially at least, each disliked the other's work.[19] Weschke was at this time beginning to find his mature voice as an artist. From the mid-1950s he had experimented with abstraction in a series of dense, heavily worked landscapes but was now in the process of moving towards a more realist and figurative way of working. In 1958–9 he had painted a monumental *Deposition Triptych* (Art Gallery of New South Wales, Sydney), possibly in Trevor Bell's studio, No.8 which was itself Baconian in its bleak vision of human cruelty, its deployment of visceral fragmented figurative forms, smeared and abraded paint and use of the triptych format. [20] In fact, although Bacon's reputation had been made with the *Three Studies for Figures at the Base of a Crucifixion* in 1944 he was not to address the triptych format again (with the exception of a single group of heads in 1953) until 1962, eighteen months after his stay in St Ives. Might Weschke's huge painting, which Bacon may well have seen in Cornwall, have been influential? For Weschke Bacon's presence and their conversations may have been decisive in confirming his choice of direction away from abstraction. In the next decade his works became more clearly figurative as can be seen works in such as *Hanging* 1961 (private collection), *Pillar of Smoke* 1964 (Tate) and the Baconesque triptych *Study for the Women of Berlin* 1969–70 (private collection).

If abstraction was in the ascendancy in St Ives in the 1950s, and held a dominant position in the 1960s, by the 1970s there was a real sense of pluralism in the art colony that was reflected by the tenants of the studios. Despite the continuing association with a particular kind of landscape-derived abstraction a number of figurative artists were attracted to the town to work, and a number, including Patrick Hughes and John Emanuel and even – very briefly – Peter Blake, were able to secure Porthmeor Studios.[21] In addition, there were a number of artists, such as Douglas Portway, Tony O'Malley, Bob Crossley and Breon O'Casey, all working in the studios, who were happy to move between figuration and abstraction in their work.

Tony O'Malley's *The Studio, Our World* 1981 is a meditation of the centrality of the artist's studio to his or her life and work. O'Malley first arrived in St Ives in 1960 to study with Lanyon and Redgrave at St Peter's Loft. He met the Canadian painter Jane Harris in 1970 and they exhibited together in his Porthmeor studio in 1972, marrying in 1973. In the painting we see the O'Malleys, who shared No.4 from 1973 to 1990, at work in their studio. The space is at once expansive but also intimate, even domestic. They are surrounded by examples of their work and the tools of their trade – pictures, paint palettes and pots of brushes. O'Malley's overcoat hangs prominently on an easel in the centre of the canvas (a motif he used on a number of occasions, for example in *The Studio No.4 Porthmeor* 1975 (private collection), as a symbolic way of evoking the presence of the artist and his daily routine of work). In the painting of 1981 the composition is unified – in a manner much indebted to Matisse's *Red Studio* 1911 (Museum of Modern Art, New York) – by a luminous blue light; the bright reflected light of sea and sky, which enters the room from the large windows to the right.

The Studio, Our World partakes of a long tradition of artists representing their own working spaces, often as a kind of surrogate self-portraiture. It makes the point that the studio is more than simply a place of work, but is the key to the artist's creativity and thus existence. Within the art colony and the community of St Ives the Porthmeor Studios – which can be understood as a microcosm of those larger contexts – occupy a similarly central position.

During this period Patrick Hughes was an important figure for the Studios. He took over No.3 from Breon O'Casey in 1973 and stayed until 1979 (retaining the studio until 1981; Roy Walker eventually moved in the following year). Hughes remembers that shortly after he arrived in St Ives Bryan Wynter, Roger Hilton and Barbara Hepworth all died, which seemed to signify the end of 'old' St Ives. After this he felt there was less sense of a prevailing orthodoxy and a kind of opening up of the scene there.[22] Hughes was a social catalyst at the studios, running a swimming club with fellow Porthmeor tenants such as the O'Malleys,

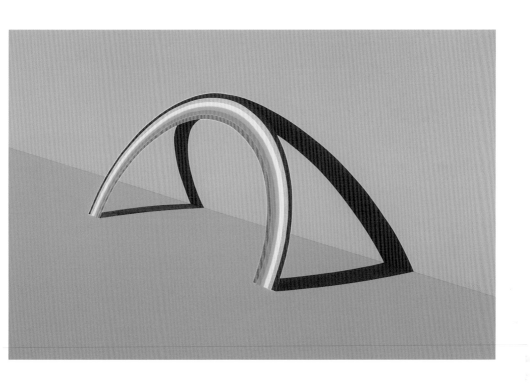

Patrick Hughes (b1939)
Leaning on a Landscape
1979
gloss on board
121.9 × 182.5 cm
Arts Council Collection,
Hayward Gallery, London
© the Artist, All Rights Reserved,
DACS 2006

and organising a darts team with Terry Frost (who by now was based in Newlyn) and his family. Steve Dove, who currently has No.4, worked as his assistant for a period.

Hughes's work is an exploration of perception and perspective. While it is essentially conceptual rather than observational he did make work responding to his new context, such as *On Reflection* 1978 (private collection), in which four toy wooden boats – purchased in one of the tourist shops typical of the town – are attached, one above the other, to a blue painted panel, so as to suggest two boats and their reflections on a calm sea. During this period Hughes also developed his use of the rainbow motif. In his work rainbows are used to explore ideas about depiction – how one 'reads' an image – and are 'oxymoronic': as in the shadow cast by a seemingly solid rainbow in *Leaning on a Landscape* 1979 (Arts Council Collection). While there are no overt references to St Ives or Porthmeor in such works one can read the preponderance of suns, blue skies and rainbows in his work of this period as somehow reflecting the seaside context. Hughes has spoken of how he found the view from the studio so compelling and perfect that one could – in a typically Hughesian conceit – have just put a picture frame around it.

Roy Ray, who arrived in St Ives in 1974 and took over the running of the St Ives School of Painting in the late 1970s, has suggested that the art colony in St Ives 'renews' itself.[23] While the work of the earlier generations of modernists such as Hepworth and Nicholson, and the so-called middle generation such as Frost and Heron continues to define 'St Ives' for many, the art colony has in fact been in a constant state of change. While the works of these artists continue to exert a powerful influence and there are many working in the region whose work is heavily indebted to their example, the presence of artists in the town such as Ray himself, Douglas Portway, Robert Floyd, Hughes and Alan Lowndes, all of whom had Porthmeor Studios, whose work makes little or no reference to the heritage of St Ives art, is testimony to such a state. The tenants of the Porthmeor Studios have reflected this state of flux. In the postwar period the studios can in fact be understood as a microcosm of the art colony in St Ives.

Throughout the period under discussion the presence of Porthmeor beach and the extraordinary and constant view of the sea continued to preoccupy the artists in the studios and to be reflected in their work. Trevor Bell has confirmed that his seemingly abstract paintings of the late 1950s and early 1960s were a direct response to the place in which he was working and the natural phenomena he was witness to every day.[24] The paintings in Bell's hugely successful Waddington's show of 1958, which included work made since he moved into No.8 in 1957, bore titles such as *Seaside*, *Sea Image* and *Cornish Coast*, and were inspired by the structure and movement of breaking waves observed on the beach. Such works did not depict Porthmeor and the sea but sublimated and abstracted from it. They were evocations of, and intimate reflections upon, form and movement coming out of a specific place and time.

In 1967 Breon O'Casey made a group of paintings depicting the view from the window of No.3. In these seascapes form is pared down to the bare essentials and colour is abstracted and freed of representational content. In one the sky is red, the sea dark blue and the beach two bands of white and ochre; in another the beach is made up of bands of pink and silver and the sky of bands of blue-brown and gold. They inevitably recall the work of Rothko but O'Casey has confirmed that he didn't know Rothko's work at this time and in fact began them as 'literal depictions' of the view.[25] In the process of making they became something else altogether.

O'Casey worked in No.3 from 1966 until 1973 and in the end, he has said, found the view too distracting. It threatened to overwhelm his work and he was forced to cover his windows in order to work.

6   Recent Developments

Until the 1960s Porthmeor beach was dominated by the tall brick building and chimney of the gasworks, which was built in 1835. In the early twentieth century it was associated with the old fishing quarter of the town and was not considered 'scenic.' By the 1920s it was beginning to be used for bathing by locals but tourists continued to use Porthminster and Porthgwidden. Nonetheless, as the town became increasingly popular as a venue for seaside holidays, Porthmeor began to be used more; a beach 'front' never developed but there were concessions established for food and drink and deckchairs. The gasworks were eventually demolished in 1958, although the gas holders remained, and subsequently Porthmeor grew in popularity.

In 1993 Tate St Ives was opened on the site of the gasworks. The possibility of establishing a gallery in the town that would show the art of St Ives had been discussed on many occasions over the previous decades. However, following the seminal exhibition *St Ives 1939–64* at the Tate Gallery in London in 1985, the idea gained momentum and support. The exhibition, curated by David Brown, was a key moment. It represented the increasing recognition of the importance of the St Ives 'school' but also its burgeoning historicisation. A number of sites were considered for the gallery but it seems particularly appropriate that the Porthmeor site was the one eventually chosen.

Tate St Ives Interior view
Photo: © Bob Berry, St Ives

The Tate St Ives building was designed by the architects Eldred Evans and David Shalev to display exemplary works of the St Ives 'school'. The forms, materials and layout of the building are explicitly designed to make reference not only to local vernacular architecture but also the modernist art of St Ives. Within the gallery the connection between the art and the building's immediate surroundings are suggested by 'spaces open to capture the seascape and roofscape present in the building and the art'.[1] Porthmeor functioned as a kind of template and the galleries are 'no larger than those of a St Ives artist's studio'.[2] Chris Stephens has suggested that the gallery 'does not just reiterate the image of the town already postulated by painted representations, it unites that imagery and the space of the town within a single construct'.[3] The extraordinary window on level two, which is one of the dominant features of the building, creates not only a symbolic but a physical link between the works of art in the gallery and Porthmeor Beach and the Atlantic outside. As Stephens argues: 'If the location of the Tate within St Ives were not sufficient, this dramatic space fixes the natural environment as a determinant in the cultural production of the town.'[4]

One problem that the presence of the Tate might have created was that St Ives would cease to be a place where art is and will be made, becoming instead a kind of heritage site. The exhibition programme has therefore attempted to address this by showing work by younger artists such as Callum Innes or Jim Lambie, and more senior figures such as David Nash, John Virtue, Richard Long or Ian Hamilton Finlay – which might suggest connections to the themes and forms of Cornish modernism – alongside major figures of the St Ives 'school' such as Hepworth, Heron, Wynter, Hilton, Lanyon, Frost, Weschke and Bell. Nonetheless, the maintenance of studio spaces that can accommodate the demands of contemporary artists is of vital

Above
Tony O'Malley (1913–2003)
The Studio, Our World
1981
Oil on board
44 × 55 cm
Private Collection
© 2006 Estate of Tony O'Malley

p85
Ged Quinn (b1963)
Cross in the Wilderness
2003/4
267 × 183 cm
Oil paint on linen
© the Artist
Photo: © Bob Berry, St Ives

importance if St Ives is to remain an important centre for contemporary art. This was partly the reasoning behind the initiation of the Tate St Ives Artists Residency scheme using No.5 Porthmeor (which became available after Patrick Heron's death in 1999), and the current scheme to redevelop the studios.

A number of small projects had been initiated by Tate St Ives in vacant studios at Porthmeor under the first curator, Michael Tooby. In 2003, however, the Director of Tate St Ives, Susan Daniel, initiated a residency scheme in collaboration with the Borlase Smart-John Wells Trust offering studio space to Cornwall-based artists. The first two artists selected to take part, Partou Zia and Ged Quinn, both painters, were each invited to use No. 5 for a period of six months and were given financial and curatorial support during that period. Each had previously been working in cramped domestic circumstances and welcomed the opportunity to develop a body of work in the large space of the studio. The fact that No.5 is one of only two studios without a window looking onto the beach created appropriate conditions for both artists, neither of whom make work based on observation and representation, and whose work might be characterised as, respectively, imaginative and conceptual painting.

Persian-born Zia's work is figurative, painterly and symbolic, exploring the 'possibility of expressing or representing a spiritual presence'.[5] She was asked to use her residency to respond to an artist in Tate's collection, and chose William Blake. She has described how being able to work on a number of pieces simultaneously and, crucially, being able to step back from her work 'was a revelation in itself'. She began her residency with a series of works that took the Porthmeor studio itself as a starting point, but while working in the studio her work underwent a transformation: 'the genre of the interior per se disappeared and a far more poetic and abstract painterly space began to emerge.'[6]

Quinn's work uses appropriation techniques – typically taking landscapes derived from paintings by artists such as Claude Lorrain, J.M.W. Turner or Caspar David Friedrich as settings for subversive interventions – to address complex moral and philosophical issues such as colonialism and genetic engineering. He has also written of the benefits of the studio and the 'huge conceptual/qualitative difference' he found compared to his previous situation, the space allowing him to develop a kind of working visual archive:

> My working method involves the evolution of idiomatic/referential elements, which become symbols within appropriated landscapes or genres. Source material... could be liberated from books and directly onto the wall in a kind of enclosed three-dimensional image and concept bank. Somehow, the individual works now began a dialogue as a group with me and between themselves. If one thing needed changing it became quickly apparent where and how and the implications for the rest of the group were visible. The space rapidly developed into an area of memory or zone of emergence.[7]

Each artist subsequently showed work from the residency at Tate St Ives.[8]

In 2004 it was decided to open the residency scheme for two years to applicants from beyond Cornwall. German-born Kerstin Kartscher was selected and showed work from the residency at Tate St Ives at the end of 2005. Nick Evans, a Glasgow-based sculptor whose seven-month residency ended in July 2006, again exhibits his new projects following the residency in October 2006.

The current group of Porthmeor tenants represent a typically diverse group. At the time of writing the tenants are Roy Conn (No.1),

Sax Impey (b1969)
Event
2004
150 × 150 cm
Mixed media on panel
© Sax Impey 2006

John Emanuel (No.2), Naomi Frears (No.3), Steve Dove (No.4), Tate St Ives Artist in Residence, Nick Evans/Jonty Lees (No.5), Ralph Freeman (No.6), Bob Crossley (No.7), Sax Impey (No.8), Richard Nott (No.9) and Bryan Pearce (No.12). The St Ives School of Painting continues to occupy No.11 and has also taken on No.10, with Roy Ray as Principal. Importantly, a number of younger artists are currently working in the studios. The painters Sax Impey and Richard Nott both make abstract work but have found ways to avoid being trapped by the legacy of St Ives modernism. Nott's blackened serial paintings resemble fired bitumen and evoke weathered natural surfaces. The carefully worked surfaces of Impey's paintings and his precise imagery take 'the seemingly impenetrable mysteries of sub-nuclear physics and mathematics as points of departure' to create 'maps of uncharted places'.[9]

The artists associated with modernist activity in St Ives did not consciously set out to follow an example set by Olsson and his associates in making work that was based (however remotely) on the direct observation of nature. However, one can argue that the experience of the Porthmeor Studios, right on the beach, with huge windows looking out onto sea and sky, meant that they could almost not avoid doing so. Olsson, through his work, personality and in particular his reputation, was a key figure for the colony and contributed greatly to the development of a place-myth for St Ives. That myth – of St Ives as a venue for the practice of landscape painting and landscape-derived abstraction – and the connections with Porthmeor were consolidated in the postwar period with the arrival of Nicholson, Frost, Barns-Graham and others, and further reinforced by the creation of Tate St Ives in the 1990s. As such the image of Porthmeor is now encoded in our understanding of the art of St Ives. It has become, by extension, emblematic of the town itself.

Notes

1   Introduction

1   Patrick Heron, letter to Robin Campbell, 4 October 1975 (Arts Council Archive) and J.P. Hodin, *Douglas Portway: A Painter's Life*, 1983, p.65. Heron's reference to thirteen studios includes the offices and downstairs work spaces of the St Ives School of Painting

2   Matthew Rowe, *Porthmeor Beach: A Century of Images*, exh. cat., Tate Gallery, St Ives 1995 [unpag.]

3   The *St Ives Weekly Summary*, quoted in Marion Whybrow, *St Ives 1883–1993: Portrait of an Art Colony*, St Ives 1994, p.30

4   John Emanuel, perhaps uniquely, claims that he came to St Ives 'for the parties'

5   In 1893 the Rate Books list three studios in the Porthmeor block, occupied by Wyly Grier, Sigisbert Bosch Reitz and Amy Llewellyn. By 1889 the number of studios there had risen to nine. Information from David Tovey

6   I am indebted to David Tovey for generously sharing the results of his research into the St Ives Rate Books. This work can be expected to illuminate this period of the art colony and correct a number of historical inaccuracies. It will culminate in a publication and an exhibition at Penlee House, Penzance in 2008

7   John Milne occupied No.2 from 1972 to 1978, and possibly also had No.8 for a short period. However, John Emanuel remembers that he used his Porthmeor Studio mainly for the storage of works, materials and casts.

8   Margaret Garlake, *New Art New World: British Art in Postwar Society*, London and New Haven1998, p.166.

9   Adrian Lewis, *Roger Hilton*, Aldershot 2003, p.95

10   Ibid, p.98

11   Mel Gooding, 'Wilhelmina Barns-Graham: A Study in Three Movements' in *Wilhelmina Barns-Graham: Movement and Light Imag(in)ing Time*, exh. cat., Tate St Ives 2005, p.9

12   Sandra Blow worked in No.9 from 1995 to 2001

13   *Paintings by Michael Snow*, exh. cat., Rowan Gallery, London 1964

14   David Lewis, 'St Ives, A Personal Memoir, 1947–55' in *St Ives 1939–64*, exh. cat., Tate Gallery, London 1985, p.25

2   Early Days

1   A.G. Folliott Stokes, 'Julius Olsson: A Painter of Seascapes', *The Studio*, vol.48, 1910, pp.274–83

2   This is borne out by the Rate Books held by the St Ives Museum. In 1898 there are nine studios listed at Porthmeor, all of which are rated at £10 per annum. except

Olsson's, which is at £25 per annum. By 1904 Olsson's studio was divided into three. Information from David Tovey

3   Borlase Smart, *St Ives Times*, 18 September 1942

4   Kenneth McConkey, *Memory and Desire*, Aldershot 2002, p.117

5   Olsson's work also suggests certain affinities with James McNeill Whistler, whose seascapes – such as *Harmony in Blue and Silver: Trouville* 1865 (Isabella Stewart Gardner Museum, Boston), *The Sea* 1865 (Montclair Art Museum) or *Violet and Silver: A Deep Sea* 1893 (Art Institute of Chicago) – are similarly devoid of compositional focus, and similarly concerned with the evocation of light and atmosphere. While Whistler visited St Ives in 1888 (in the company of Walter Sickert and Mortimer Menpes, see Menpes's account of the visit in *Whistler as I Knew Him*, London 1904), two years before Olsson arrived, it is interesting to note that a number of Olsson's students, including Mary McCrossan, (who occupied No.9 Porthmeor in the 1920s and 1930s, running her own painting school) produced distinctly 'Whistleresque' work. Nonetheless, ultimately Olsson's kind of painting rejects both Romanticism and Aestheticism and foregrounds a form of Realism; observation and visual fact, is the key.

6   N.G. [Norman Garstin] in *The Studio*, vol.6, no.33, December 1895

7   Stokes, op cit.

8   McConkey 2002, pp.108–9

9   Nina Lubbren, *Rural Artists' Colonies in Europe 1870–1910*, Manchester 2001, pp.115–16. Lubbren's development of the 'place-myth' thesis (see in particular chapter 6, 'Painting Place-myths') is more complex than I have been able to reflect here

10   From the *St Ives Weekly Summary*, quoted in Marion Whybrow, *St Ives 1883–1993: Portrait of an Art Colony*, St Ives 1994, p.22

11   Austin Wormleighton, *Morning Tide: John Anthony Park and the Painters of Light*, St Ives 1900–1950, Stockbridge 1998, p.35

12   Ibid

13   David Tovey's recent research shows that Olsson's stay at Porthmeor was probably shorter than has previously been reported; he may have had the great Porthmeor studio for as little as three years and not the twenty-five suggested elsewhere

3   Between The Wars

1   Quoted in Virginia Button, *Christopher Wood*, London, 2003, p.40

2   Letter to her Rachel Hodgkins, dated 19 November 1914, in Linda Gill (ed.), *Letters of Frances Hodgkins*, Auckland 1993. It is interesting to note that Hodgkins refers to No.7 as huge: it is in fact the smallest studio in the Porthmeor block

3   Letter to Rachel Hodgkins, dated 8 December 1914, in Gill 1993, p.299

4   Letter to Isabel Field, dated 16 November 1915, in Gill 1993, p.312

5   Letter to Rachel Hodgkins, dated 6 January 1915, in Gill 1993, p.300

6   Letter to Rachel Hodgkins, dated 10 Feb 1916, in Gill 1993, p.313

7   Letter to her Rachel Hodgkins , dated 17 Feb 1915, in Gill 1993, p.303

8   One of her students, Agnes Drey, eventually settled in the town and occupied No.2 Porthmeor, 1942–57

9   Other artists at Porthmeor during this the period include Arthur Hayward, Marcella Smith, Mary McCrossan, Hugh Gresty and Claude Barry

10   *St Ives 1939–64*, exh. cat., Tate Gallery, London 1985, p.149

11   Leonard Fuller in *Borlase Smart, Memorial Exhibition*, exh. cat., Penwith Society, St Ives 1949

12   Borlase Smart, *The Technique of Seascape Painting*, London 1934

13   In 1985 a single work each by Park and Smart was included in the Tate Gallery's seminal survey of the modern movement in St Ives, *St Ives 1939–64*

14   From the earliest days of the art colony an important phenomenon, in which the studios played a central part, was Show Day. Every March, before the paintings were due to be sent up to London for submission to the Royal Academy and other exhibitions, artists would open up their studios to visitors and show the work they were sending. The Newlyn artists also opened their studios and the events in the two towns were carefully timed so as not to compete with each other. Artists with larger studios, such as those at Porthmeor, would often invite others to show with them. From quite early on Show Day was a major event not only for the art colony but also for the people of St Ives. It was important in creating a situation where the local people accepted the artists in their midst, as well as promoting the activities of those artists.
Frances Hodgkins was in St Ives in 1902 and described the event as 'show day, the great day of the year'. She saw fifteen studios occupied by thirty-two artists but was very critical of the work she saw there, singling out Olsson and Arnesby Brown as the best. She recalled that 'It was great fun going round – the studios were hidden in the queerest places – down dark subterranean passages, up chicken ladders – in old boat houses up sail lofts – anywhere where they could get a whitewashed wall & a top light.'
By 1924 Show Day was a celebratory event for the whole community and the *St Ives Times* began publishing official lists of exhibitors. From 1919 until 1928, when the St Ives Society of Artists began to use No.5 as an exhibiting space, those exhibiting regularly at the Porthmeor Studios on show days include Claude Barry, Alfred Hartley, Lindner, Marcella Smith, Arthur Meade, Frances Ewan, George Bradshaw, Hugh Gresty, and Arthur Hayward

15   Peter Davies, 'Notes on the St Ives School', *Art Monthly*, No.48, July/August 1981

16   The history of the St Ives Society of Artists has been dealt with in detail elsewhere. See in particular David Tovey's, *George Fagan Bradshaw – Submariner and Marine Artist – and the St Ives Society of Artists*, Tewkesbury 2000 and *Creating a Splash*, exh cat, Penlee House Gallery and Museum and tour, 2003

4   After The War

1   Borlase Smart Memorial Fund Prospectus, Arts Council Archive

2   The debt was eventually written off in 1999

3   It seems now very likely that without Philip James's vision, his timely intervention and skilful mobilising of the Arts Council's resources, that the studios would have been lost. The SISA still had a huge – and potentially impossible – sum of money to raise and had practically exhausted local resources. James must therefore be recognised as a key figure in the survival of the studios

4   P.B.Williams to Philip James, 9 September 1949, Arts Council Archive

5   Charity Commission Register. The name of the trust was changed in 1995 to The Borlase Smart-John Wells Trust to take account of the generous bequest by artist John Wells, of his studio in Newlyn

6   Gerald Cock to Gabriel White, 25 March 1968, Arts Council Archive

7   Ben Nicholson to Philip James, 20 March 1951, Arts Council Archive
8   Louise Walsh to Philip James, undated, Arts Council Archive
9   Gerald Cock, letter to Philip James, 16 January 1952, Arts Council Archive
10 Ben Nicholson to Philip James, 24 May 1949, Arts Council Archive
11 Ben Nicholson to Philip James, 4 June 1949, Arts Council Archive. The commission
    was for two concave panels for the *SS Rangitania* of the New Zealand Shipping
    Company
12 Quoted Sarah Jane Checkland, *Ben Nicholson: The Vicious Circles of his Life and Art*,
    London 2000, p.283.
13 Ben Nicholson to Philip James, 12 November 1949, Arts Council Archive. One of
    these paintings was almost certainly *December 1949 (poisonous yellow)* (Galleria
    Internazionale d'Arte Moderna di Ca' Pesaro, Venice)
14 Quoted in Peter Khoroche, *Ben Nicholson: Drawings and Painted Reliefs*, London
    2002, p.70
15 Ben Nicholson to Philip James, 15 November 1949, Arts Council Archive
16 Khoroche 2002, p.70
17 Ibid., p.71
18 Ibid., p.70
19 Patrick Heron, 'Ben Nicholson' in *New Statesman and Nation*, 16 May 1952
20 Nicholson was awarded the Pittsburgh International award in 1952 for *December 1949
    (poisonous yellow)* and the first Guggenheim Painting Award in 1957 for *August 1956
    (Val d'Orcia)* (Tate)
21 Ben Nicholson to Philip James, 30 May 1958, Arts Council Archive

5   Abstraction and Figuration

1   Patrick Heron to Philip James, 19 June 1958, Arts Council Archive
2   Patrick Heron to Philip James, 23 June 1958, Arts Council Archive
3   Patrick Heron, 'American Artists from the EJ Power Collection/Roger Hilton' (1958)
    reprinted in Mel Gooding ed., *Patrick Heron: Painter as Critic: Selected Writings*, London
    1998, pp.150–153
4   In this year Heron wrote: 'My main interest, in my painting, has always been in colour,
    space and light … and space in colour is *the subject* of my painting today to the
    exclusion of everything else. But the space must never be *too* deep, or the colour
    too flat. Each painting has to adjust depth to surface in a new and unique manner.'
    (Statement in 'Two Reception Rooms', *Architecture and Building Magazine*, October
    1958). Four years later he wrote: 'It is obvious that colour is now the *only* direction in
    which painting can travel. Painting still has a continent left to explore, in the direction of
    colour' ('A Note on my Painting', 1962)
5   Quoted in Mel Gooding, *Patrick Heron*, London 1994, p.160
6   See for example, the endpapers of Mel Gooding's monograph
7   I am indebted to Katharine Heron for her observations on the way her father used his
    studio
8   Lawrence Alloway, *Nine Abstract Artists*, London 1954, p.12
9   Redgrave, primarily a sculptor, was also something of an entrepreneur. He also had a
    Piazza studio, which he worked and slept in and his wife Mary 'Boots' Redgrave ran a
    B&B from their house, 1 Island Square.

10   Michael Peppiat, *Francis Bacon: Anatomy of an Enigma*, London 1996, p.181

11   Francis Bacon to Harry Fischer, 19 October 1959, Marlborough Fine Art Archive

12   William Redgrave, Journal; I am indebted to Chris Redgrave for permission to quote from William Redgrave's journals

13   Ibid

14   Ibid

15   There are a number of interesting anecdotes concerning works that Bacon left behind. One of these has Tony O'Malley, who used No.3 after Bacon, finding a number of works and swapping one with Dai Vaughan for a sheepskin coat. Another has Bill Featherstone using a number of Bacon sketches on hardboard to roof a henhouse.

16   Redgrave Journal

17   Ronald Alley, *Francis Bacon*, London 1964. The paintings are *Lying Figure* 1959 (private collection), *Sleeping Figure* 1959 (private collection), *Study from Portrait of Innocent X by Velasquez* 1959 (Tai Cheung Holdings, Hong Kong), *Head of a Man* 1959 (private collection), *Miss Muriel Belcher* 1959 (private collection) and *Head of a Man – Study of a Drawing by Van Gogh* 1959 (private collection)

18   Illustrated in *Francis Bacon*, exh. cat., Gemeentesmuseum Den Haag, The Hague 2001, p.73. Tate has two preparatory drawings for this painting. See also Martin Harrison, *In Camera, Francis Bacon; Photography, Film and the Practice of Painting*, London, 2005, for an examination of the implication of Bacon's stay in St Ives.

19   Information from Karl Weschke

20   Redgrave was also working on a deposition in 1958

21   Peter Blake's proposed tenancy was keenly debated by the Trustees as it was felt that i) he did not need the studio, and ii) he might not make full use of it. In the event he was offered the tenancy as it was felt that the presence of such a major, established artist could only be beneficial for the art colony. Blake barely used the studio and gave it up before the year was out

22   Patrick Hughes, conversation with the author, 11 November 2004

23   Roy Ray, conversation with the author, 10 September 2004

24   Trevor Bell, conversation with the author, March 2005

25   Breon O'Casey, conversation with the author, 7 September 2004

6   Recent Developments

1   David Shalev and Michael Tooby, *Tate Gallery St Ives: The Building*, St Ives 1995, p.28

2   Ibid

3   Chris Stephens, 'On the Beach: Art, Tourism and the Tate St Ives', in Micheala Giebelhausen, *The Architecture of the Museum: Symbolic Structures, Urban Contexts*, Manchester 2003, p.109

4   Ibid, p.112.

5   *Partou Zia in Conversation with Sara Hughes*, Art First, London 2004, p.1

6   Partou Zia, unpublished report on Tate St Ives Artists' Residency, 2004

7   Ged Quinn, unpublished report on Tate St Ives Artists' Residency, 2004

8   See *Partou Zia*, exh. cat., Tate St Ives 2003, and *Ged Quinn: Utopia Dystopia*, exh. cat., Tate St Ives 2004

9   James Burleigh in *Sax Impey: Events*, exh. cat., New Millennium Gallery, St Ives 2004

Afterword

Porthmeor Studios and Fishing in St Ives
BRIAN STEVENS

There is an old yet very true adage that oil does not mix with water, except that is, at St Ives, as there on the very edge of the ocean this is exactly what has and does still occur. Today, the sea of the North Atlantic Ocean laps the wall of studios that has contained one of the most historically renowned colonies of artists in the Western Hemisphere. There, for a century and more, artists have plied their craft with skill, resulting in many of the finest oil paintings to grace leading art gallery walls worldwide. Yet, there beneath those selfsame studios, fishermen pursue their respective calling, storing their fishing gear, besides making and repairing nets; men of the sea united with painters in oil and working in harmony since the latter decades of the nineteenth century. In what manner then did such a relationship come about and how does this unique mixture of oil and water continue to blend in the twenty-first century?

To answer this question we must resort to nature; through countless centuries of wave and wind action, a sandy isthmus had built up from Porthmeor Beach to the Island and over to the Meadow, near where Tate St Ives stands today. Especially with northerly gales, huge amounts of wind-blown fine sand resulted in great sandbanks, proving impossible to build there. That was, however, to be remedied in the late eighteenth century with the construction of a vast sea wall.

The Porthmeor Wall
The story behind the building of this wall commences in 1762, when John Knill was appointed as Collector of Customs. Born at Callington,

with St Ives family connections, he quickly became established and well respected. A man of vision, he was arguably the greatest benefactor to St Ives of that period. Via his contacts, Knill had invited John Smeaton, marine architect, to visit the port with the view to creating a plan for a larger and safer harbour, which Smeaton duly devised. Work began on a new pier (and subsequently sea wall) in 1767. Presumably, as a reward for services rendered in steering this project to fruition, Knill was awarded Mayoral office at the commencement of construction of the aptly named 'Smeaton's Pier'.[1]

The 'Porthmeor Wall', as it is known, when completed must have presented a formidable battlement to those who viewed it; and so it should do, it needed to prevent billions of grains of wind-blown sand that had to be repelled from encroaching further on 'Porthia', the former name of the harbour area. Little wonder then, that this wall had but a single opening in its entire length; positioned at its most eastern end, its purpose was to allow access for a small rowing boat, presumably for coastguards and pilots to assist in rescue at sea. Dated 1824–8, the earliest maps pinpointing this area are from a collection held at the Cornwall Record Office. These show the line of Porthmeor Wall, completed in 1801, with the sandbanks reaching in as far today as the Sloop Inn Car Park, Carnglaze and Quay Street.

---

1   An extract from Mr John Knill's will dated 1809:

During the residence of upwards of twenty years at St Ives, where I was Collector of the Customs and served all offices within the borough from constable to mayor, it was my unremitting endeavour to render all possible service to the town in general, and to every individual inhabitant; and I was so fortunate as to succeed in almost every endeavour I used for that purpose, particularly in respect to the building of their *wall and pier*, and in some other beneficial undertakings; and it was my wish to have further served the public by effecting other public works, which I proposed and which will, I dare say, in time be carried into execution…

The Cellar Development

St Ives was built for its fisheries; the principal fish, the smallest and most numerous, being the humble pilchard. Although much investment had been made concerning the industry since the completion of Smeaton's Pier in 1770, the opening years of the nineteenth century were difficult ones for the pilchard fisheries in Cornwall, not least in St Ives. Hostilities commencing in the 1790s put England at war with France and Spain, preventing the procuring of French salt for the fish curing process; difficulties on the high seas also prohibited the successful export of the finished product to Mediterranean countries. But, during the brief peace of 1802–3, and with Smeaton's wall completed the previous year across Porthmeor Beach, certain local fisheries sought permission of the freeholders to build on this wall; properties for an extension of fishery interests, predominantly for the curing of pilchards and associated trades, commenced in great earnest[2]. By the 1830s, the entire length of this wall, secured from the drifting sands, was occupied by substantial cellars to service the local pilchard or 'seine'

---

2   The great landowners were Stephens of Tregenna, Praed of Trevethoe, Lelant and Mornington, owner of many estates and an absentee landlord. From deeds we learn that the site in question was then in the legal ownership of Sir Christopher Hawkins, Bart, until he died 6 April 1829. It is presumed that with a subsequent new freehold owner, further building continued along the line of the wall, quickly followed by mass construction of properties on the sandbanks, with other freeholders, including Stephens, Praed and Mornington following suit. By consulting *The Mornington Estate Papers* a Conveyance dated 3 May 1889 [CRO GHW/12/1/5/1] the exact date and names of the owners of one of the first properties to be built on this section of wall is revealed:

also all that piece or parcel of land situated on the south side of Porthmeor Beach in the Borough of St Ives aforesaid, lately held under a lease granted in the year 1811 to Thomas Bolitho and William Bolitho, but now (1889) unoccupied, bounded on the west by premises used as a cooperage belonging to Messrs. Bolitho, on the east by certain fish cellars and houses belonging to the vendors, now under lease to William Paynter, on the south by a public street known as Back Road, and on the north by Porthmeor Beach...

Porthmeor Washday, 1908
© Cornwall Study Centre, Redruth
Image shows Porthmeor Wall with single access at one end

Porthmeor 1 January 1952
Artists Studios almost engulfed with wind blown sandbanks
© Brian Stevens

fisheries[3]. Such was the growth of the industry, that these numerous huge fish cellars and lofts were constructed.

However, not all had been well, as war on the high seas recommenced during 1803, and continued until April 1814. By this date, the situation apparently had led a certain speculator to bankruptcy, but the following excerpt from a resulting sale advert in the *Royal Cornwall Gazette* 10 July 1814, does throw a little light on the extent of these properties:

> …that large and commodious Fish Cellar, Salt House and Lofts, Most conveniently situated in St Ives, late the Property, and in the occupation of Mr. Richard Gyles, a Bankrupt, but now in the occupation of Mr. John Stevens and Mrs. Couch. Also, For the Remainder of a like Term, determinable on the decease of three young Lives, All that newly-built Cooperage and Yard, also late the Property, and in the occupation of the said Richard Gyles.

---

3   S. Winfred Paynter writing in November 1927, described the process of 'seine' fishing:

A great change has taken place in the fishing industry of St Ives since my young days, partly caused through a change in method, and partly because, for some unknown reason, the fish have altered their breeding and feeding grounds, and no longer frequent the neighbourhood of St Ives Bay in the numbers that darkened our waters a century ago. At the present time the fishermen seek fishing grounds at considerable distances away, and catch their fish by means of a '*drift-net*', in the meshes in which the fish become entangled; but when I was a boy, and for many years after, pilchard fishing was done, not by the drift-net process, but by the '*seine-net*' process, which was a much more complicated, but also a much more profitable business.

Seine fishing may be described as fishing in shallow waters; by means of a net about twelve hundred feet long and ten fathoms deep, a portion of the sea was encircled and enclosed, and its content pulled ashore. The control of the process lay in the hand of the '*seine-owners*', who met frequently and apportioned the sea amongst themselves by an ingenious plan which, although it did not exclude the excitement of chance, did at least eliminate all suspicion of favouritism.

Although evidence of the *Fish Cellar, Salt House and Lofts* has yet to be traced, they were most probably handy to where the new cooperage and yard were situated. From a St Ives Poor Rate Ledger for 1839 a number of cooperages can be located, but the only one that had a yard that suits this description, plus the date, was the one mentioned in the 1889 lease already quoted, which presumably was subsequently purchased by Messrs Bolitho as it was adjoining their cellar premises.

On closer inspection, the construction sustaining Porthmeor Studios was built between eighteen and twenty feet in height on the original 1801 wall. The support inside was of granite pillars set approximately twelve to fifteen feet off the wall and to a height of approximately eight feet. With a timber lintel positioned on the pillars and with flooring joists set from the wall to the lintel, a timber studwork wall was erected with a pitched roof in line with the wall. The roof being scantle-slated[4] and support studwork was also upright slated.

Beneath, on the ground floor, a beam press was affixed to the wall for pressing the cured pilchards, whilst a lean-to slate roof, or 'penthouse', from beneath the window line, afforded a weather protected area for the pilchards to be bulked in salt for curing.

The floor was 'caunsed', being laid with sea-worn small stones, these 'bowlies', derived from the adjoining beach. Above was the net loft, the driest area, where the extensive seine nets were made, repaired and stored between seasons. Next there was built a salt house and cooperage. To the rear of the cellar, as with others along the wall,

---

4   Varying sizes of slate from the ridge to the base of the roof, each slate diminishing by an inch in length but the width is random.

was a sand bank, a full twelve feet in height that was eventually stabilised by retaining walls that afforded other properties to have cellars to the north side of lane behind, today named Back Road West.

Over the years, my interest has increased in the time schedule over which 'Downlong' – the local term for the community of lower St Ives, encircled by the sea wall – was built. Various records reveal 1801 is really its birth date, as one traces the dates of the properties emerging on the Porthmeor Wall. (This is similar to commencing a jigsaw by doing all the straight-edged bits first and then filling in the middle, which is usually the hardest!) Nevertheless, by the 1880s, all the land reclaimed from the shifting sandbanks inside the sea wall had been developed, with every building – including the sea wall edifice, which became the Porthmeor Studios – in one way or another, being associated with that particular fish, the pilchard.

The trades and crafts, which were everyday occupations of literally hundreds of workers, particularly in the Downlong locality, included shipwrights and the supporting trades of that great industry: sawyer, blacksmith, anchor smith, mast and spar-maker, pulley and block-maker, rope-maker, sail-maker, tinsmith and cooper. All required premises in which to carry out these crafts and were mainly at ground level, adjacent to the waterfront. The rope-makers had their respective ropewalks at the Warren, above the harbour and, later on, parallel to the 'Back Roads' running behind Porthmeor Wall. Sail-makers carried out their trade in huge sail lofts fronting the harbour.

The Development of the Net Lofts
The craft of net-making demanded dry locations and ground-floor premises such as cellars were entirely unsuitable. Today, modern fibres are completely unaffected by cellar conditions, unlike the cotton twine

which required curing preservative to enable it to last longer. It was the expansive net lofts that were the most numerous in the first and second floors of properties over fish curing cellars.

In the main, net making was a cottage industry and mostly carried out by the women folk. Those performing this skill went by the trade name of 'beetster', which literally means the 'maker of nets' in Cornish. In many of the Downlong cottages, the kitchen was a workroom and in practically every homestead, there was a net in the process of being made in a corner of the room. Nets were of various sizes in mesh, depth and length, and when finished would be taken to the net loft to be 'set'. Such an undertaking demanded a lengthy area and so special premises were built to accommodate this procedure.

The largest lofts were for the seine nets, stop nets and tuck nets. All three were large and exceptionally weighty as all three types had leads affixed to the foot ropes at varying distances. Today, many of these lofts are converted for accommodation or other purposes and often named as 'Sail Lofts'; a misnomer as seine net lofts never accommodated any sails. The reason quite simply being that seine fishing boats were powered by oars and not by sail.

Those net lofts were very heavily constructed with iron pillars to support the joists and floors, with first floor vertical slated studwork and roof timbers with its slate work. Upon this floor each net would be placed separately. It was common practice in some company net lofts to write the name of the seine net above on the principal timber of the roof, as each seine net had a name given to it for identification purposes when engaged in pilchard seine fishery. The seine net would be put into the same named seine boat. This was by Act of Parliament in the case of the St Ives fishery.

Many traces of the loft complexes and the fish-curing cellars – at that time great industrial premises – have disappeared. Fortunately, aerial photography came about before all identity of these buildings was lost in the labyrinth of twentieth century development. The St Ives' Poor Rate Ledgers of the period 1840–60, again reveal just how many cellars and net lofts there were over the lower part of the town.[5] The changing fate of the pilchard industry consequently reshaped the town.

Porthmeor Studios

By the 1850s, the Downlong building boom was over. From 1880, the fisheries were in decline and the mode of curing pilchards was changing. Economics stated that the labour intensive hand-bulking of fish was too costly. To overcome this, in certain cellars excavated deep in the sand, huge tanks were constructed either with brick then rendered, or of shuttered mass concrete, made from Fore Sand gravel. By shovelling salt and then fish into these tanks alternately, the process was much quicker and cheaper, although it has been recorded that the quality of the finished product was not the same.

St Ives at this time was an evolving artists' colony and the demand for studios was great, especially along the Porthmeor Wall as the north facing

---

5   One difficulty however is that the exact locations are not revealed. For example, the largest entries are for the Back Roads. This has been confirmed as being to either side of this main road, across Downlong from the Porthmeor sea wall to the Harbour foreshore. Confirmation and elimination of those former industrial properties has been painstakingly arrived at by studying the amount of rates paid for certain properties. Firstly, if one makes a note of the property's description, such as cellar and loft, together with its amount for rates due, then what are at this present time known to have been substantial properties can be identified first. Then it is elimination after the confirmation. And so it goes on. One difficulty is that every few years what started off as just one property being called 'New Cellar' increases to three or four with such a description by the 1850s, and as I expect you have surmised nearly all are in 'Back Roads'.

A seine-boat and her crew
making sure all is well with
the huge seine-net that they
had just shot
1905
© St Ives Museum

Seine-boats with their nets
and oars moored by the Quay
at St Ives ready for the next
day to await the arrival of
the shoals of pilchards
1905
© Comley Collection

Seine-boats loading aboard
seine-nets from West Pier,
St Ives
1905
© Comley Collection

studios were especially favoured for their light. With the fishing industry at St Ives in decline, this resulted in redundant net lofts. These were sought after as primitive living accommodation, from which artists could paint the ever-changing pattern of life that continually proceeded right in front of their window, particularly those that faced the harbour. The net lofts over the great fish curing cellars adjoining Porthmeor Wall however, were facing north, so great glass windows were placed in the wall itself and skylights inserted in the roofs, to let the light directly into the converted studios.

One mode of painting was to capture in paint or pen as many of the subjects as possible outdoors, or *en plein air* as it was called, during fine weather. Then to invite the people that made up the scene into the studios when the weather was unsuitable, for either artist or people involved. The latter meaning the slack times during the fishing calendar seasons when, particularly those associated with fishing, could earn a pence or two by posing. These 'models' would wear the same clothes as when the subject matter was first outlined on the canvas; background and foreground could be painted indoors during spells of poor weather conditions, with the canvas repeatedly being taken to the original location to ensure an authentic reproduction.

There was immense scope for a conversion of purposely-designed studios and, as mentioned in a conveyance of 1889, the site of the Porthmeor Studios was unoccupied. Early in the 1890s, a large first-floor area was constructed and partitioned off to provide studios. Beneath this was formed a huge cellar, and with the largest tanks in Downlong, they were instantly utilised for pilchard curing.

There is an assumption that those tanks might have been constructed during the mid 1880s, with lean-to roofs to protect their contents; it is believed also that the net lofts were converted for the pressing of

Artist painting in the harbour, with fishermen and boats
1920s
© St Ives Museum

'Dandy Dick'
1900
© Comley Collection

pilchards, either by a beam press, but more likely by the more 'modern' screw press. In the *Comley Collection* of photographs and glass slides of St Ives, (1885–1910), there is a wonderful photograph of local fisherman 'Dandy Dick' mending nets in a converted beam pressing loft, which can clearly be seen. A concurrent canvas existed of a scene of women working in a press loft that contains screw presses. It is a possibility that either the photograph or painting could be of the loft being considered.

The *St Ives Weekly Summary 9 August & 6 September 1902*, contained an advert that gives details of the sale of this entire block of property. Both converted studios and cellars, as well as tanks, are given in much detail, including their then present occupiers.

> Lot 2. – All those FIVE NEWLY-ERECTED ARTISTS STUDIOS at Porthmeor, St Ives, and now in the respective occupations of Messrs. Fox, Adams, Brook, Douglas and Lindner. The studios are also recently built and are very commodious, with good approach, and all of them with a northern aspect and splendid sea views.

> Lot 3. – All that CELLAR or STORE situated at Porthmeor aforesaid, under the said studios, measuring about 74 feet 6 inches in length, 56 feet 6 inches in width, and 10 feet in height,– with several well constructed tanks for curing fish – late in the occupation of Mr George Williams deceased.

> Lot 4. – All that STORE situate at the eastern end of the said cellar, measuring about 27 feet 6 inches in length, about 24 in width and 10 feet in height, now unoccupied, with the studio over the same, in the occupation of Mr Bosh-Reiz.

> Lot 5. – About 50 Tons of FISH SALT.

Porthmeor Wall Cellar and Net Loft
c1815

Porthmeor Studios and Fish Tank Cellar
c1895

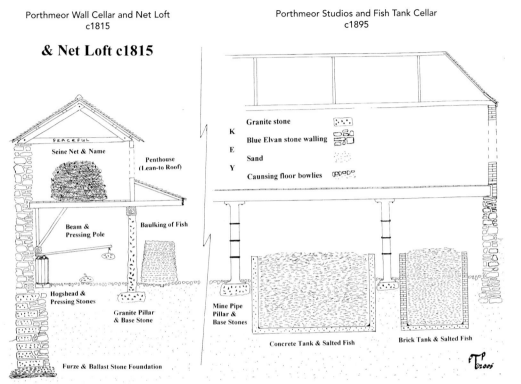

& Net Loft c1815

PEACEFUL

Seine Net & Name

Penthouse
(Lean-to Roof)

Beam &
Pressing Pole

Baulking of Fish

Hogshead &
Pressing Stones

Granite Pillar
& Base Stone

Furze & Ballast Stone Foundation

K
E
Y

Granite stone

Blue Elvan stone walling

Sand

Causning floor bowlies

Mine Pipe
Pillar &
Base Stones

Concrete Tank & Salted Fish

Brick Tank & Salted Fish

**Line drawing,
plan of the wall, cellar, loft,
tanks and studios**
© Tre Pol Pen

The advert reveals the purpose and usage for which the store building was originally constructed, namely a salt cellar, with a section of the 'new studios' being that of a former net loft. Never was there a sail loft, as references have been made to this property. [6]

Just over one hundred years ago in 1905, the cellar tanks were full of curing pilchards that were taken either in Messrs Bolitho's or Rouncefield Brothers' seines. Today, these same tanks contain fishermen's nets and gear; both ground floor and the first floor of these premises continue to have long-standing occupiers, still pursuing their respective calling as artist or fisherman. Unity and respect for one another is an additional hallmark for this last remaining corner of old St Ives.

There is little of the original Porthmeor Wall remaining, the majority being the frontage of this property. The wall's foundations, which have stood the test of time, are still stable and secure, and the future for both artists and fishermen alike within the Porthmeor Studios complex will continue in harmony. The fisher-folk with their boats and nets, the artists with their easels and palettes have long been living together at St Ives. This closing remark brings home how personal it is to the writer. My maternal great grandfather was so friendly with a one well-known artist, Louis Grier, that the youngest of his sons was named Louis Monroe Grier Stevens when born in the year 1901. Grier was a successful painter in oils and Stevens, a most successful fisherman of the sea, oil and water mixing then as now. Long may this unique blending continue to the benefit of One and All.

BRIAN STEVENS is a local historian and Honorary Curator of the St Ives Museum

6   St Ives Poor Rate Ledgers for 1902 state that the owners were Messrs Bolitho and the tenant the Williams family. The salt cellar was at this time also used as stables and the cooperage (not mentioned in the sale) was owned and worked by George Williams who had died earlier in that same year.

Appendix 1
Artists using the Porthmeor Studios 1949–2005

No.1

Wilhelmina Barns-Graham	1945 – March 1963
Roy Conn	March 1963 – present

No.2

Agnes Drey	1942 – July 1957
Lucy Walsh	Sept 1957 – April 1964
Marion Grace Paul	April 1964 – Oct 1965
Una Shaw-Lang	Oct 1965 – June 1972
John Milne	1972 – 78
Vacant	1978 – May 1982
Peter Blake	May 1982 – Oct 1983
John Emanuel	Oct 1983 – present

No.3

Cdr George Bradshaw	1940 – Dec 1958
(sub-letting to Wilhelmina Barns-Graham during the war and to Dorothy Lawrenson in 1945)	
William Redgrave/St Peter's Loft	Dec 1958 – Aug 1962
(including sub-let to Francis Bacon Sept 1959 – Jan. 1960)	
Alan Lowndes	Aug 1962 – June 1966
Breon O'Casey	June 1966 – 1973
Patrick Hughes	1973 – 1982
Roy Walker	May 1982 – 2002
John Mitchell	2002 – 05
Naomi Frears	2005 – present

No.4

Leonard Richmond	c1948 – March 1951
Terry Frost	April 1951 – March 1963
(including sub-lets to John Forrester)	

Patrick Dolan | March 1963 – Jan. 1968
Dai Vaughan | 1968 – 73
Tony and Jane O'Malley | June 1973 – Sept 1990
Steve Dove | Jan 1991 – present

No.5

Borlase Smart | 1945 – 7
David Cox | 1948 – 9
Ben Nicholson | June 1949 – May 1958
Patrick Heron | June 1958 – 1999
Tate St Ives Residency | 2002 – present
Partou Zia | March – Sept 2003
Ged Quinn | Sept 2003 – Aug 2004
Kerstin Kartscher | Oct 2004 – Sept 2005
Nick Evans | Dec 2005 – July 2006
Jonty Lees | Aug 2006 – May 2007

No.6

Frances Ewan | c1944 – 62
Cedric Rogers | Aug 1962 – 1968
Tony O'Malley | March 1969 – June 1973
Roy Walker | 1973 – May 1982
Steve Dove | May 1982 – Jan 1991
Louise McClary | Jan 1991 – March 1995
Ralph Freeman | 1995 – present

No.7

Frances Ewan | before 1944 – Dec 1957
Gwen Leitch | Jan 1958 – 62?
Jeffrey Harris | 1963 – Jan 1970
(including sub-lets to Peter Ward for six
months in 1964 and L.R. Ulsley in 1965)
S.M. Peter | Jan 1970 – March 1972
Roy Walker | March 1972 – 1973
Bob Crossley | Oct 1973 – present

No.8

Lucy Walsh | 1939 – Sept 1957
Trevor Bell | Sept 1957 – 62

(including sub-lets to Roger Hilton for one
year c.1957–9 and possibly Anthony Benjamin,
Michael Snow and Karl Weschke in 1958)

Michael Snow	Aug 1962 – April 1968
Douglas Portway	c1968 – Jan 1984
Robert Floyd	Jan 1984 – 2002
Sax Impey	2003 – present

No.9

Alixe Jean Shearer Armstrong	c1938 – June 1983

(including possible sublets to Isobel Heath
and Robert Adams c.1975)

Karl Weschke	Jan 1984 – Sept 1993
Sandra Blow	March 1995 – 2001
Richard Nott	2003 – present

No.10

Hyman Segal	1948 – 2004
St Ives School of Painting	2005 – Present

No.11

*Includes upper studio, lower studio
and office space*

St Ives School of Painting	1938 – present
Leonard Fuller, Principal	1938 – 73
Marjorie Fuller (nee Mostyn), Principal	1973 – 79
Roy Ray, Principal	1979 – present

No.12

*An additional studio converted from two
lofts below the School in February 1952*

William Redgrave	1952 – 8
John Barclay	Dec 1958 – Dec 1964
Mary Williams	Dec 1964 – Aug 1970
James Whitlock	Sept 1970 – June 1973
Bryan Pearce	Oct 1973 – present

Appendix 2
Glossary

'Porthia'   Cornish *Porth* = sandy bay 'of Saint Ia'

'Porthmeor'   Cornish *Meor* = great 'sandy bay'

'Carnglaze'   Cornish *Carn* = rock and *Glaze* = blue or green.

'Beetster'   trade persons name, one, principally females,
                    who made nets.

Definitions from *Old Cornwall* Vol. XI. No. 11, Page 525. Autumn 1996.

Bibliography

Books and Articles

Ronald Alley, *Francis Bacon*, London 1964

Lawrence Alloway, *Nine Abstract Artists*, London 1954

Janet Axten, *Gas Works to Gallery: The Story of Tate St Ives*, St Ives 1995

Denys Val Baker, *Britain's Art Colony by the Sea*, London 1959

W.H. Bartlett, 'Summer Time in St Ives, Cornwall', *Art Journal*, 1897, pp.292–5

Iain Buchanan, Michael Dunn and Elizabeth Eastmond, *Frances Hodgkins: Paintings and Drawings*, London 1995

Virginia Button, *Christopher Wood*, London, 2003

Katie Campbell, *Moon behind Clouds: An Introduction to the Life and Work of Sir Claude Francis Barry*, St Helier 1999

Sarah Jane Checkland, *Ben Nicholson: The Vicious Circles of his Life and Art*, London 2000

Tom Cross, *Painting the Warmth of the Sun: St Ives Artists 1939–1975*, Tiverton 1984

Tom Cross, *The Shining Sands: Artists in Newlyn and St Ives 1880–1930*, Tiverton 1994

Peter Davies, 'Notes on the St Ives School', *Art Monthly*, July/August 1981, pp.3–8

Peter Davies, *After Trewyn: St Ives Sculptors since Hepworth*, Abertillery, 2001

Brian Fallon, *Breon O'Casey*, Aldershot 1999

Margaret Garlake, *New Art New World, British Art in Postwar Society*, Yale 1998

NG [Norman Garstin] 'Studio Talk', *The Studio*, 1895 onwards

Micheala Giebelhausen, *The Architecture of the Museum: Symbolic Structures, Urban Contexts*, Manchester 2003

Inga Gilbert, *Reflections on Paintings by Douglas Portway*, Edinburgh 1993

Linda Gill (ed.), *Letters of Frances Hodgkins*, Auckland 1993

Mel Gooding, *Patrick Heron*, London 1994

Mel Gooding ed., *Patrick Heron: Painter as Critic: Selected Writings*, London 1998

Lynne Green, *Wilhelmina Barns-Graham: A Studio Life*, Aldershot 2001

Louis Grier, 'A Painter's Club', *The Studio*, vol.5, 1895, pp.110–14

Martin Harrison, *In Camera, Francis Bacon; Photography, Film and the Practice of Painting*, London, 2005

J.P. Hodin, *John Milne: Sculptor*, London 1977

J.P. Hodin, *Douglas Portway: A Painter's Life*, London 1983

Michael Jacobs, *The Good and Simple Life: Artist Colonies in Europe and America*, Oxford 1985

Vivien Knight (ed.), *Patrick Heron*, London 1988

Peter Khoroche, *Ben Nicholson: Drawings and Painted Reliefs*, London 2002

Adrian Lewis, *Roger Hilton*, Aldershot 2003

David Lewis et al., *Terry Frost*, Aldershot 1994

Jeremy Lewison, *Ben Nicholson*, Oxford 1991

Jeremy Lewison, *Karl Weschke: Portrait of a Painter*, Penzance 1998

Nina Lübbren, *Rural Artists' Colonies in Europe 1870–1910*, Manchester 2001

Kenneth McConkey, *British Impressionism*, Oxford 1989

Kenneth McConkey, *Memory and Desire: Painting in Britain and Ireland at the Turn of the Twentieth Century*, Aldershot 2002

E.H. McCormick, *Portrait of Frances Hodgkins*, Auckland 1981

Mortimer Menpes, *Whistler as I Knew Him*, London 1904

Alison Oldham, *Everyone Was Working: Writers and Artists in Postwar St Ives*, Tate St Ives/Falmouth College of Art Fellow 2002

Jack O'Sulivan, *A Celtic Artist: Breon O'Casey*, Aldershot 2003

Michael Peppiat, *Francis Bacon, Anatomy of an Enigma*, London 1996

Roy Ray, *Art About St Ives*, St Ives 1987, (reprinted 2006)

Roy Ray, *Observations on a Journey*, St Ives n.d.

Leonard Richmond, *The Art of Landscape Painting*, London 1928

David Shalev and Michael Tooby, *Tate Gallery St Ives: The Building*, London 1995

John Slyce, *Patrick Hughes: Perverspective*, London 1998

Borlase Smart, *The Technique of Seascape Painting*, London 1934

A.G. Folliot Stokes, 'The Landscape Paintings of Mr Algernon Talmage', *The Studio*, vol.42, 1907, pp.188–93

A.G. Folliot Stokes, 'Julius Olsson: A Painter of Seascapes', *The Studio*, vol.48, 1910, pp.274–83

David Sylvester, *Looking Back at Francis Bacon*, London 2000

David Sylvester, *About Modern Art*, London 1996

Michael Tooby, *Tate Gallery St Ives: An Illustrated Companion*, London 1993

David Tovey, *George Fagan Bradshaw – Submariner and Marine Artists – and the St Ives Society of Artists*, Tewkesbury 2000

David Tovey, *WHY Titcomb, A Newlyner from St Ives*, Tewkesbury 2003

Austin Wormleighton, *Morning Tide: John Anthony Park and the Painters of Light, St Ives 19001950*, Stockbridge 1998

Laura Wortley, *British Impressionism: A Garden of Bright Images*, London 1988

Marion Whybrow, *St Ives 18831993: Portrait of an Art Colony*, St Ives 1994

Partou Zia in Conversation with Sara Hughes, London 2004

The essay in this publication by Brian Stevens, 'Porthmeor Studios and Fishing in St Ives' has been compiled and enlarged upon by the author of the following published articles:

Tre Pol Pen, *Where are the Net Lofts and Sail Lofts Today?* St Ives Times & Echo 23 & 30 January 2004

Tre Pol Pen, *1905 St Ives' Last successful Pilchard Seining Season*, St Ives Times & Echo 19 & 26 August 2005

Tre Pol Pen, *Porthmeor Studios courtesy of Messrs. Knill and Smeaton*, St Ives Times & Echo 13 January 2006

Exhibition catalogues

Wilhelmina Barns-Graham: Movement and Light Imag(in)ing Time, Tate St Ives 2005

Francis Bacon: Paintings 1959–60, Marlborough Fine Art, London 1960

Francis Bacon, Tate Gallery, London 1985

Francis Bacon: Working on Paper, Tate Gallery, London 1999

Francis Bacon: A Retrospective, Yale Center for British Art, New Haven, and touring 1999

Trevor Bell, Waddington Galleries, London 1958

Trevor Bell: A British Painter in America, Florida State University Museum of Fine Arts, Tallahassee 2003

Trevor Bell: Beyond Materiality: Paintings and Drawings 1967-2004, Tate St Ives, 2004

Sandra Blow: Space and Matter 1958–2001, Tate St Ives 2002

Bob Crossley: 45 Years of Painting, Penwith Galleries, St Ives 1987

Emanuel Phillips Fox 1865–1915, National Gallery of Victoria 1994
Paintings by Patrick Heron 1965–1977, University of Texas at Austin
    Art Museum, Texas 1978
Patrick Heron, Tate Gallery, London 1998
Roger Hilton, Hayward Gallery, London 1994
Sax Impey: Events, New Millenium Gallery, St Ives 2004
Ben Nicholson, Tate Gallery, London 1993
Tony O'Malley: Painter in Exile, Ulster Museum, Belfast 1984
Tony O'Malley: A Personal Choice by Vera Ryan, Crawford Municipal
    Art Gallery, Cork 1994
An Irish Vision: Works by Tony O'Malley, The Phillips Collection,
    Washington, DC 2000
John Anthony Park, Montpelier Studio, London 1993
John Anthony Park, Montpelier Sandelson, London 1995
Ged Quinn: Utopia Dystopia, Tate St Ives 2004
William Redgrave 1903–1986, Roy Miles Gallery, London, 1998
Memorial Exhibition of the Work of Borlase Smart, Penwith Society of Arts,
    St Ives 1949
Borlase Smart, Penwith Gallery, St Ives 1981
Paintings by Michael Snow, Rowan Gallery, London 1964
Michael Seward Snow: A Retrospective,
    Gordon Hepworth Gallery, Exeter 1993
Karl Weschke, Kunstammlung Gera 2001
Karl Weschke: Beneath a Black Sky: Paintings and Drawings 1954–2004,
    Tate St Ives 2004
Partou Zia: Entering the Visionary Zone, Tate St Ives 2003

Artists of St Ives and Newlyn, Whitechapel Art Gallery, London 1902
Post-Impressionism: Cross-currents in European Painting, Royal Academy
    of Arts, London 1979
St Ives 1939–64, Tate Gallery, London 1985
British Art in the 20th Century, Royal Academy of Arts, London 1987
St Ives, Hyogo Museum of Modern Art, Kobe 1989
Porthmeor Beach: A Century of Images, Tate Gallery, St Ives 1995
Creating a Splash: The St Ives Society of Artists, Penlee House Gallery and
    Museum, Penzance, and touring, 2003
Art & the 60s: This Was Tomorrow, Tate Britain, London 2004

Index

First published 2006 by
order of the Tate Trustees
by Tate St Ives

in association with
Tate Publishing
a division of Tate Enterprises Ltd
Millbank, London SW1P 4RG

www.tate.org.uk/publishing

This book is the second in the
Tate St Ives RESEARCH Series

Texts by   Ben Tufnell
                  Brian Stevens and
                  Susan Daniel

© The authors and Tate 2007
All images courtesy of artists and lenders
as credited
All photography © the photographers

Series Editor   Susan Daniel

Edited by   Judith Severne
                  Sara Hughes
                  Kerry Rice and
                  Arwen Fitch

Design   Groundwork, Skipton

Repro and print   Jigsaw, and Eden Print

This project has been supported by
Tate St Ives Members and Tate Members

British Library Cataloguing in
Publication Data

A catalogue record for this book
is available from the British
Library

ISBN-10: 1 85437 695 0
ISBN-13: 978 185437695 4

Front cover
Ben Nicholson (1894–1982)
June 4–52 (Table form)
1952
158.8 × 113.7 cm
Albright Knox Gallery, Buffalo,
New York
© Estate of Ben Nicholson,
All Rights Reserved
2006 DACS, London